LOVE

in the

SECOND

ACT

JEREMY P. TARCHER/PENGUIN

a member of Penguin Group (USA) Inc.

New York

LOVE

in the

SECOND ACT

*True Stories of Romance,
Midlife and Beyond*

ALISON LESLIE GOLD

JEREMY P. TARCHER / PENGUIN
Published by the Penguin Group
Penguin Group (USA) Inc., 375 Hudson Street, New York, New York 10014, USA • Penguin
Group (Canada), 90 Eglinton Avenue East, Suite 700, Toronto, Ontario M4P 2Y3, Canada
(a division of Pearson Penguin Canada Inc.) • Penguin Books Ltd, 80 Strand, London
WC2R 0RL, England • Penguin Ireland, 25 St Stephen's Green, Dublin 2, Ireland (a division
of Penguin Books Ltd) • Penguin Group (Australia), 250 Camberwell Road, Camberwell,
Victoria 3124, Australia (a division of Pearson Australia Group Pty Ltd) • Penguin Books
India Pvt Ltd, 11 Community Centre, Panchsheel Park, New Delhi–110 017, India • Penguin
Group (NZ), Cnr Airborne and Rosedale Roads, Albany, Auckland 1310, New Zealand
(a division of Pearson New Zealand Ltd) • Penguin Books (South Africa) (Pty) Ltd,
24 Sturdee Avenue, Rosebank, Johannesburg 2196, South Africa

Penguin Books Ltd, Registered Offices:
80 Strand, London WC2R 0RL, England

Most Tarcher/Penguin books are available at special quantity discounts for bulk purchase for
sales promotions, premiums, fund-raising, and educational needs. Special books or book
excerpts also can be created to fit specific needs. For details, write Penguin Group (USA) Inc.
Special Markets, 375 Hudson Street, New York, NY 10014.

Library of Congress Cataloging-in-Publication Data

Gold, Alison Leslie, date.
Love in the second act : true stories of romance, midlife and beyond / Alison Leslie Gold.
p. cm.
ISBN 1-58542-466-8
1. Love in middle age—Case studies.   2. Love in old age—Case studies.   3. Man-woman
relationships—Case studies.   4. Middle-aged persons—Psychology—Case studies.   5. Older
people—Psychology—Case studies.   I. Title.

HQ1059.4.G68   2006   2005053868
306.73'40844—dc22

Printed in the United States of America
1   3   5   7   9   10   8   6   4   2

Book design by Stephanie Huntwork

While the author has made every effort to provide accurate telephone numbers and Internet addresses
at the time of publication, neither the publisher nor the author assumes any responsibility for errors,
or for changes that occur after publication. Further, the publisher does not have any control over and
does not assume any responsibility for author or third-party websites or their content.

"I'm afraid I have some very bad news," the doctor explains. "You're getting older and you don't have all the time in the world left."

"Oh, that's terrible," cries the patient. "How long have I got?"

"Ten," the doctor says unabashedly.

"Ten?" the patient inquires. "Ten what?"

"Nine . . ."

Contents

LOVE

in the

SECOND

ACT

While waiting in line to buy tickets at the Loews movie theater on Broadway at Nineteenth Street, my friend Barbara asks if I'm in the mood to be fixed up.

"Fixed up?"

"Fixed up! You know, fixed up on a date. I know a Jewish folksinger that's divorced. I also know a magazine editor who liked your last book."

If a heart can be likened to a violin, now that my last relationship is over and the beautiful music has stopped, I can't imagine that music will ever again resonate from these strings.

"You must be kidding," I respond, giving her a fishy look.

The line inches forward.

"I don't know what you're waiting for," Barbara says combatively. "You're not getting any younger."

I bristle. "Where were you when F. Scott Fitzgerald said that there are no second acts in American lives?"

"I guess I was having one. Where were you when Oscar Wilde, or maybe it was Samuel Johnson, said that a second marriage is the triumph of hope over experience?"

Barbara's posture is faultless; her voice has an air of soft aridity. She squeezes my arm. "In back of my addled brain, I seem to remember something about how life begins at forty. Or is it fifty? Look at me. I didn't get together with Warren until I was pushing fifty. As you well know, at that point I'd been around the block more than a few times."

Today—the first cold blowy day of autumn—I'm wearing a new wool coat with the collar turned up. There's dampness in the lambent air. Shaggy clouds dangle in the sky. Barbara's not much older than Madonna. She always brightens whatever she wears with some arresting splash of color. Today she's wrapped a mango-colored scarf smartly around her throat. Her cheeks are pink and warm to my lips when I kiss her hello or good-bye. We've been friends for nearly twenty years.

"Fitzgerald was no fool," I add in a steely tone.

"At least ungird your loins!" she suggests. "I'm living proof that Fitzgerald was an idiot. You should hear my friend Beatrix White *kvell*. In the middle of her life, after about a million failed relationships, when she was about ready to throw in the towel, Bea found Mark. Or Mark found Bea. Indecorous exteriors be damned!"

"Okay. Okay. Okay, " I say to shut her up. And that's where the traveling symposium that has become this book began.

I'd been licking my wounds after the breakup of a twelve-year relationship. Looking for some bulwark in life, I'd come back to New York after twenty years out west. New York—the city where I grew up—is Tara. Though I didn't feel prepared for the rigors of city life, I'd come home. Shortly after my conversation with Barbara, through a set of coincidences, I met Charlotte, a career woman who married for the first time at sixty. When she showed me the wedding announcement that had appeared in the *New York Times*, I noticed in it the mention of a biographical update she'd sent to her alumni newsletter that said: *No trips taken in years; no children; obviously no grandchildren, no husband.*

Then, she went on a two-week Smithsonian-sponsored trip to Ireland. That first morning on the tour bus she sat next to Mike Chamberlain, a retired radio announcer from San Francisco. They began to talk. One thing led to another and—

On January 23, they were married in the creaky wood-paneled chapel of the Convent of the Sacred Heart on Fifth Avenue. . . . Like the actress Katharine Hepburn, Charlotte Mary Cassidy is partly regal, partly tomboyish. Now 60 and a learning specialist at the Trinity School in New York, Miss Cassidy wears her long gray hair in a Hepburnesque bun and loves fresh air so much she opens the windows even in winter.

. . . Like her many roommates, Miss Cassidy also expected to marry young, but instead she remained single. "I wasn't surprised that she never married," Gabriella Befani Canfield, a friend, said. "Some of us, of our generation, are what I call women in between. We are much too independent and outspoken to be the right women for men of our generation."

. . . When Charlotte left for Ireland last summer, she told friends she hoped to bring back some pretty dish towels. Instead she brought back the towels and a new love. "What are the chances of this happening at our age?" Maudie Davis, a guest at

her wedding, said. "A friend of mine died last week of cancer. Here is one contemporary who has died and the other is getting married. In your sixties, it can go either way."

My ponderings percolated to the point that I took up Barbara's challenge. I began instigating conversations with people (like Charlotte and myself) who'd reached, or passed through, that juncture of midlife when the knack for self-deception has weakened and the face in the mirror is no longer quite our own.

I'd had my moment in the mirror one hazy afternoon shortly after my return to New York, when I caught a glimpse of myself reflected in a window of Gristede's supermarket on Eighth Avenue and did a double take because the visage returning my look was not quite the one that had always been there. In my case the sensation was a little like being aboard an airplane that encounters turbulence and realizing that I'm helpless to stop it. That feeling, along with my move east, my breakup, and the dismal state of the world, were the catalysts that got me to begin to muse on my life, my career, and the stasis I was in.

After publishing five books relating to World War II and the Holocaust, I realized that the time had come for me to write about life not death, romance or comedy if possible, rather than savagery and evil, love not hate. Since I was responding to love stories both bitter and sweet, I also began clipping wedding announcements and bits and pieces that I chanced on. I labeled a file folder "Into the Good Night," and slid all the clippings inside.

In the interviews with lovers that I was conducting, I was turning into a latter-day Kinsey. Surprisingly often, those I questioned became enthusiastic and offered to relate their own experience or one that belonged to someone they knew. Over the course of what became a stormy and snowy fall and winter, while traveling or at home, while eating and drinking, I took part in an extremely engaging, often surprising, series of dialogues on love and age.

Although sex and romance among those who are middle-aged or older is often viewed with gooey eyes through an offensive *Golden Pond*-like lens, the experiences that were described to me were passionate, mad, tempestuous, complex, and bittersweet. The people in these interviews had all, in one way or another, moved beyond that moment in the mirror and decided to go on and search for, or open themselves, to love. (Or, in the case that love isn't an opening-out but a closing-in, to close themselves around love.) To "rage against the dying of the light." The age range in this collection goes from forty-three through ninety-seven; the younger subjects are children of the fifties and boomers in midlife, the older are lively octogenarians and nonagenarians nearing their final curtain. Though many had experienced disappointments and failures, they are vital folk who hospitably invited me into their private lives. And this is what struck me the most as I began to assemble twenty-five of these interviews and various other materials: In the second act, love and partnering is not only possible, but can be hot and delicious, life-giving and hope-giving. Both passion and heartbreak are as profound at fifty as they were at twenty.

From the sociological side, we're well aware that life expectancy has lengthened considerably and, as Eva S. Moskowitz writes in *In Therapy We Trust* about this moment in time, *happiness [has become the] ultimate goal, and psychological healing is the means.* We've entered an era of changed possibilities demanded by older, more active, more vigorous, physically fit, sexually empowered women and men. If being who and what you are isn't enough, for men who choose to give nature a little assistance, there's Viagra, Levitra, Cialis (tempting men with what Robin Williams, in his comedy act on turning fifty, laughingly calls "the dick from hell") and for women there's testosterone, HRT, synthetic pheromones and more.

A suitcase full of life-enhancing pharmaceuticals is available: There are memory enhancers, hormone replacements, bone boosters, serotonin elevators, wrinkle creams, stress and depression relievers, and various rejuvenators. There's also surgical help to offset the physical ravages of time: makeovers, renovations, augmentations. Perhaps these artificial enhancers have influenced our expectations of what post-midlife should offer? Perhaps they are false hopes? They can be embraced or not, the choice is there. The limits of childbearing or adopting have expanded; gay as well as transgender communities have joined the mainstream; celebrities retain their glamour and sexuality as they trudge toward the sunset. (Actor Helen Mirren: "I was never gorgeous. Ever. When you're young you want more than anything to be beautiful, but as you get older, you don't have that desperate need and it's a great feeling." Jack Nicholson to Diane Keaton in *Something's Gotta Give*: "I'm sixty-three years old and in love for the first time in my life.")

Post-feminist sexuality prizes boldness. *Sex and the City* is just the most famous of many examples. Mating practices have changed; resources that provide romantic connections are a growth industry that includes online dating services, matchmakers, personals columns, speed dating, mixers and so on. Learning, traveling and sharpening the mind are de rigueur for the retired. The model for love from the Middle Ages through to this century is young love: Dante and Beatrice, Romeo and Juliet, the romantics who mostly died young, rebel without a cause, too fast to live, too young to die, and so on. This long-established model has been breaking down. Take Marquez's *Love in the Time of Cholera* and Ha Jin's *Waiting* and Kundera's *Immortality*. Finally, there are romantic role models older than Dante and Beatrice, older than Romeo and Juliet, who are more like Antony and Cleopatra.

That is the real revolution!

Approaching a "big" birthday, Paul Theroux, the novelist and travel writer, returned to Africa where he had spent his young manhood. He writes in *Dark Star Safari*:

> *What all older people know, what had taken me almost sixty years to learn, is that an aged face is misleading. I did not want to be the classic bore, the reminiscing geezer, yet I now knew: the old are not as frail as you think, and they are insulted to be re-garded as feeble. They are full of ideas, hidden powers, even sex-ual energy. Don't be fooled by the thin hair and battered features and skepticism. The older traveler knows it best: in our hearts we are youthful, and we are insulted to be treated as old men and burdens, for we have come to know that the years have made us more powerful and streetwise. Old age is Strength.*

Over the course of my search, certain similarities and themes rise like steam over our coffees and conversations. Although each story is unique, I've organized this offering into nine sections in an attempt to highlight significant patterns—each encapsulating a few of the themes my interlocutors have underscored in relation to their coupledom.

IN LOVE WITH LOVE: No matter how much heartbreak or grief women and men have endured in past relationships, they'll usually have another go at love.

LIBIDO: Human beings never stop being sexual. Getting older doesn't have to mean getting colder.

180-DEGREE TURNS: It's possible to radically change career and house and ambition and lifestyle in the second act.

COMFORT AND STABILITY: Degrees of intimacy and steadiness not accessible earlier in life may be achieved in the second act.

BLIND LOVE: Some couples, who've remained together through both acts, through many changes, experience love as immutable.

SECOND VIRGINITY: Certain subjects discovered that they were wrong when they thought there would only be one "first time." Love keeps changing and there are always new firsts.

HOMECOMING: Sometimes there's an experience of returning to an earlier self in later life.

DETERMINATION: Certain subjects demonstrated that almost anyone who truly wants love and sex, if willing to work at it, can find it. In other words, if act one has been screwed up, or if fate has been unkind, perseverance pays off.

TIME *IS* ON YOUR SIDE: My subjects demonstrated that no matter how old, shopworn, tainted, dogged by disappointment one is, it's never too late. There's time. Ironically, many of these couplings would not have been thinkable in the same way a generation back.

Making these trips and having these conversations became a pleasure indeed. I was entertained and charmed by these human targets into which the beautiful naked blind winged boy with the bow has been shooting his sharp arrows. In a few cases, either by request or because I thought it best, the names of the subjects have been changed and identifying facts blurred. For those of us who are in the wings garnering the willingness to step onto the stage, I'll say this: If a lonely heart can be likened to a violin whose music has stopped, in these many interviews, I heard the sound of music resonate again and again from its strings.

ACT TWO, SCENE ONE

In Love with Love

On my way to an interview I have another moment in the mirror. This, my replete reflection in the bulletproof plastic dividing the front and the backseat of a grubby yellow cab. While the driver speaks nonstop into his mobile phone in a language I can't identify, and the windshield wipers whack, we're stuck in traffic on Seventh Avenue going south. The sky is the color of oyster shells; a cold monotonous rain has been falling for three days and nights. I've been straining my eyes roughing out questions—Is a desire for love something we get over like the flu? Is love something that can be peeled like an onion? When I look up, I'm dismayed to see a woman in midlife with strands of gray in her hair, with a cherry-red, yellow and orange-colored scarf around her neck. The face is far from old, but—then again—it's far from young. Lines from Cavafy's "Candles" cross my mind:

> The days of the future stand before us
> Like a row of little lighted candles—
> Gold and warm and lively little candles.

The days past remain behind,
A sad line of snuffed out candles;
The nearest are still smoking. . . .

The face is aging. I wonder, "Has my heart grown cold? Have I coarsened? Why does a mirror reverse right to left and not up to down?" During that first moment in the mirror a few years before, I'd been struck by soft lines like doilies around my eyes, a slight droop in the skin. Now I observe owl eyes, a neck that's going stringy, graying hair with little volume. I'm not sure if I'm looking at my face or the aggrieved face of a stranger.

I hope I won't be late for my appointment. How much more rain can fall? Umbrella-toting people crossing at the crosswalk look as if they're sleepwalking. For better or worse, the acrimonious national election is finally over, the city's exhausted, the temperature's supposed to drop below zero tonight, or so it's been predicted. If it does, it'll be hell when the puddly streets freeze up. I haven't suffered a fierce Eastern winter in twenty years, and am daunted by the prospect of slipping on a swatch of black ice and falling on my ass.

"The interesting thing about committing yourself to one person is it's like deciding you're going to spend your life in Turkey. So you never go to China."

At one point toward the end of the 1981 film *My Dinner with Andre*, directed by Louis Malle, the costar Andre Gregory says to his dinner partner, Wallace Shawn, "I realized that what I wanted most in my life was to always be with Chiquita." Viewed in retrospect, the line becomes bitterly poignant because at that moment in Andre's life he hadn't an inkling that ten years later, after thirty-three years of marriage, fate would take his beloved wife Chiquita from him.

Andre

I pick Andre up at his apartment on an atmospheric street in Greenwich Village. The rain has stopped, there's a purple fringe of light left in the sky. Waiting at the door while he gets his winter coat, I can see a blown-up photograph of Andre, Wallace Shawn and Louis Malle on the wall. On another wall, close to the ceiling, my eye is drawn to the photograph of a beautiful woman.

"That's Chiquita," Andre explains, as he buttons his coat.

We walk a short distance from his apartment to a little Italian place on West Fourth Street. Thankfully the rain has stopped. The wet, leafy streets are shining. Though over twenty years have passed since *My Dinner with Andre*, his patrician looks and kind eyes haven't changed at all. Theater director, actor, writer, teacher, national treasure, Andre's currently preparing a film version of Ibsen's *Master Builder* in a new translation by Wally Shawn.

Andre orders a chopped salad and herb tea. I order a double espresso. If this wasn't New York, I'd have thought our waiter—who has a face like Napoleon—curt. I ask Andre to tell me if it's too hard to talk about Chiquita. Looking into my eyes, with a

LOVE IN THE SECOND ACT   15

sweet expression on his face, he says with a New Yorkish accent, "I can talk about anything."

"After the death of your Chiquita, did you leave behind much of your life?"

"Yeah. I was kind of ruthless when my wife died. I suddenly had this peculiar opportunity that I didn't want, this painful opportunity to do anything I wanted with my life. It was almost like being twenty years old."

"Did your friends change?"

"Well . . . yeah. For the most part the only friends from the past life that I stayed close to were Wally Shawn, Richard Avedon and a few of the actors I'd worked with. Otherwise I just walked out of my life and I disappeared."

"Why?"

"I'd say that the two of us, on a certain level, lived an inauthentic personal life. In other words, I was doing some of the most radical theater of the sixties and seventies but I was living in a nice apartment on the Upper West Side with a doorman. My friends were people I went to Harvard with . . . not artists."

He sold his apartment right after that realization.

"Did you want to live?"

"I always wanted to live. I have tremendous life energy and of course my calling—my vocation—is a part of that. My daughter was part of an ashram in upstate New York. I went up to the ashram. There was this amazing paradox. On the one hand being in grief and terrified about what the hell I was going to do, on the other hand stepping into this intense, ecstatic . . . I was both grieving and in ecstasy. The guru there gave me—more or less—an impetus to life, toward new life. I've never been funnier in my life than I was at that time."

Our beverages arrive. "Were you surprised at yourself? If you were directing a man who had just lost the great love of his life . . ."

"Ha, ha. One of the hallmarks of my work is ambiguity, so it may not have seemed so off if I were directing that man. He might well understand that you can be two extremes at the same time."

"Maybe one was healing the other?"

The waiter returns with Andre's salad.

"Educating the other."

"Have you been as funny since?"

"I don't think so."

"How long did you stay at the ashram?"

"I kept going back over four years. People confuse the spiritual and the religious. In the religious you can have a set of beliefs which are cerebral. The spiritual is where you're experiencing the divine in your blood cells. It's almost like having sex around the clock."

"Had you been able to access these feelings in the first part of your life?"

"No. I probably wouldn't have gotten there if I hadn't been in such great pain and great confusion. If you've just lost somebody, living on an ashram like that is much nicer than living in New York City where death is the ultimate failure."

"Explain that."

"We live in such a materialistic culture that death is just a failure. You become a little bit of a pariah. I remember I'd go to restaurants with a book 'cause I didn't know how to cook and people would come in who knew me and I could tell that the moment they saw me it was, 'Oh, that guy.' They'd kind of look away and go to their table."

"Besides the ashram, what other sort of Band-Aids did you try?"

"I did have an extraordinary therapist at the time."

"When you started thinking about women, were you looking for another kind of woman?"

"When it happened after a few years, the women I started going out with were absolute poison. It was like going back to twenty . . . having to have my face shoved into all this stuff I'd never really dealt with. My own particular poison is women who are somewhat abused, a little distant, removed, unavailable, wounded, the absolute opposite of the woman I'm married to now."

"You must have been an eligible widower."

"And how. I discovered what most people know, dating is a horror."

"Is it?"

"Yes. I've always loved women. When I was a little kid I always used to play with the girls. I wasn't a jock. I always feel quite awkward with men."

"You're not the towel-snapping, locker-room type?"

"Yeah. I've always liked women. It's been reciprocal. I certainly felt the need to have a woman in my life."

"Did you want to reproduce Chiquita, try to find someone like her . . . a duplicate?"

"Yeah. Definitely."

"Did you ever feel that she was sending someone to you?"

"I think in a funny way she sent me my present wife 'cause the way I met Cindy was I wrote a beautiful, peculiar play in verse about Chiquita's illness . . . our marriage . . . our last days together and one of the musicians who was working on the play accidentally introduced me to Cindy. He wasn't trying to fix her up or anything."

The Napoleon-like waiter walks over to our table and asks me, "Would you like another espresso?"

When I tell him to bring me a regular coffee, he gives me an icy look, challenges, "What's wrong with the espresso?"

"It was fine but I'm trying to slow down my caffeine intake."

He shakes his head and darts away.

"What's the title of the play?"

"*Bone Song.*"

"Did you know right away there was something about Cindy?"

"Yeah. Yeah. Within days. She's a very good filmmaker, very joyful by nature, which would not have interested me in the past. What was fun was that neither of us thought it would turn into a romance for about a week."

"You'd just be playmates?"

"Yeah. She's wonderful company. We met out in Bridgehampton. We went for walks on the beach, went to the movies, talked a lot."

"Had she been married before?"

"Nope. She had a couple of seven-year relationships."

"Uh oh! How long have you and Cindy been together?"

He laughs. "We're over that hump. I was worried about that. No. We're fine. You know what's interesting, we almost never fight. We get irritated with each other once a year. There's no conflict. It's not because we're hiding a lot of stuff, we're just very playful. In that way we let the other know if there's something that annoys us."

"What does she look like?"

"She's petite. I don't like to say what somebody looks like. She's fairish but not blond. She has the radiance of a sunflower, the spirit of a sunflower."

I need to digest that comment and pause in my questioning. I don't really think of sunflowers as radiant.

"You say you wouldn't have been interested before in someone like her?"

"No. She was too happy. I liked trouble. You know the thing that's always so fascinating about the poison we're attracted to is that it comes in a new package, new wrapping. You think, Oh, this is different. You get the wrapping off, it always turns out to be the same thing. We're drawn like bees to honey, very often to what's going to be painful. It's because of this guru and my therapy that I grew out of the necessity to be in pain."

The waiter brings the coffee. I take a sip.

"It's espresso!"

"Yes!" he responds defiantly.

I take another sip and realize he was right to bring me espresso. It's what I really wanted though I hadn't realized it. He sees my satisfaction and gives me an "I told you so" look before he turns away.

"Why do you think we want pain?" I ask with curiosity.

"Many of us think that life has to be hard. When, in fact, if you're a working, successful artist, one of the most privileged groups in the entire world, we're able to be children all our lives, doing what we want to do. We have an enormous amount to be grateful for if we can just get beyond that necessity to live in troubled waters."

"Do you still go to therapy?"

"No. I went back to do a little therapy when Bush won the election."

"It was a horrific election."

"It's infuriating. I just turned seventy. I'm having the time of my life. My children, God willing, are well, my marriage is wonderful, I'm doing some of the best work I've ever done. On a purely selfish level there's something awful about those people fucking up. During the election campaign I rang four hundred twenty-five doorbells in Pennsylvania. It was seventeen steps up to every door, seventeen down. Physically and emotionally I felt drained afterwards. I've been struggling since the election with how to be joyful given the state of the world. With no end in sight."

"It's possible that we could be surprised. I try to remember things that turned on a dime. Like you did, you got a new life. You didn't expect it."

"It's very peculiar, I know."

"Do you feel guilty for being happy?"

"I think this is worse than Reagan."

"You didn't expect the result of this election?"

"I think what's been unleashed in Iraq, we're not going to see an end to in our lifetime, I'm afraid. The big challenge is how to stay joyful. I think Che Guevara said, 'The greatest weapon of a revolutionary is hope.' We can't afford in these times the luxury of despair. My goal would be to not deny the horror of what's going on—we're torturing people—at the same time, to be able to somehow live my life ecstatically. My role model is the rabbi who married Cindy and I. He lost all twelve members of his family, I think he was in Auschwitz when he was a child, and he is a complete ecstatic. He says he is living the ecstatic life for the others who were not able to do it. So I don't think we should feel guilty."

"So you're enjoying this time of your life, Andre?"

"I'm loving it. I have never loved my life so much. I've started painting, something I never did in my entire life. I love my work. I love my hobby. The last years have been the most delightful I've ever spent. You know when you're younger you do worry about everything. You worry about your career, your kids. I'm trying to do a film of Ibsen's *Master Builder*. I've been working on it for seven years. Have you seen *Vanya on Forty-second Street*?"

Shamefully, "No."

"You should see *Vanya*. See it on a big screen. I'd love to make *Master Builder* into a film. I don't know how many more works I'll do in my lifetime. Actually, in some ways, I'm much more excited about my paintings than my theater work. Doing something you don't know how to do is very exciting."

"In that case, maybe it's time for me to write poetry?"

"Great to do that. So yes . . . I don't have a complaint in the world. My only complaint is the probability that I don't have fifty more years. Cindy and I are living on the Cape. We have two cats, Felix and Puccine."

"Did you have other pets before?"

"Dogs. I just spent four or five months on the Cape. There's something interesting about one's natural self. I have always been somebody who's supposed to be in nature only I didn't know it. The life on the Cape . . . going to watch the sunset . . . watching the moon . . . the natural beauty . . . the painting is related."

"It's nurturing. It's opium, the beauty of nature. Natural beauty is always enough."

"That's right. The only place I can find here is to go up to the Metropolitan and look at the paintings."

"I accidentally find it lying in my own bed. I can watch the moon make its journey across the sky from my bed."

I signal for the bill.

"It's funny what you're calling this book because you know in the theater, especially in film, act two is supposed to be the trouble act. Act three is where it gets resolved."

"Do you think life is a three-act play? Your own?"

"Probably two acts. Of course in life it isn't likely you'll get more than two acts. I remember when Simone de Beauvoir's book came out about older people and sexuality in the fifties. The thought that people over forty had sex was so radical. As a young theater person I went to what was the greatest theater in the world, that of Bertolt Brecht in Berlin. I spent a lot of time there. He'd just died. His widow Helene Weigel was running things. She was about fifty-five at the time. She was incredibly sweet to me. It only occurred to me years later that perhaps she wanted to have an affair. I didn't think that women of that age had sex. It's certainly saddening because I think that would have been quite a ride."

"Do you feel separate from youth?"

"They do seem very foreign. . . ."

We fight over the check.

"One of the privileges of working in the theater is that you work with people of all ages."

"I also like people of all ages. But there's much I don't relate to. Sometimes I feel like it's not my world anymore."

He refolds his linen napkin and puts it on the table.

"If Chiquita could come back today she wouldn't recognize the world in a funny way. There was no e-mail, no cell phones. If she saw Cindy editing a film on a computer, she wouldn't know what the hell it was."

"It's incredible."

"And it's only twelve years."

Twelve years! Blink. A lifetime. I begin to button my coat, wrap my striped scarf around my neck and comment, "There are some things our grandchildren will never know, like dial phones."

"I try to stay divorced from the technology. I know how to get a fax and how to send one. I like to talk to people on phones."

"Funny you haven't lived abroad. I can see you living in Europe or India."

"I knew Europe in the fifties when Europe of the fifties was not that much different than Europe of the thirties. If I was blindfolded and dropped into Paris or Berlin I'd know where I was by the smell. Now I go rarely."

"In some ways everywhere's like one big L.L. Bean catalog."

"So much of Europe has become Americanized. If you go, it's not as though you left home. The whole concept of developing yourself wasn't known in the fifties. I was absolutely sure I wouldn't remarry. It's been an amazing experience to be married again . . . to be married to somebody if I'd met her even ten years ago I might not have given her a second look because I've changed so much. I've changed partly as a result of that long marriage, partly as a result of that illness, partly as a result of my therapy. The interesting thing about committing yourself to one person is it's like deciding you're going to spend your life in Turkey. So you never go to China and you have no idea whether or not you like China. Living in Turkey is quite an experience. Then suddenly you change enough and the world changes enough. You can have a completely second life. I don't think I would recognize myself as I lived. The person who's living now and the person in the last marriage are simply two completely different people."

We stand outside the restaurant. "So if the twenty-five-year-old Andre came into this restaurant and saw you, what would he think of you? Or the thirty-five-year-old?"

"He might be a little envious. He probably wouldn't have had the nerve to live the life I'm living."

That weekend I rent *Vanya on 42nd Street* and am struck when Vanya, played by Wallace Shawn, assures his sister that in spite of so much misery, "We'll live through a long row of days . . . and we'll bear up." How apt, I thought.

"I am mindful that my spouse has a Medicare card"

You're very political and out, aren't you?" I ask Tom Kirdahy, a lawyer in his forties who has been working in a law firm to provide direct, free legal service to people living with HIV and AIDS.

"Yeah. In every way."

"How did the election affect you?"

"It was crushing."

"Did you have hopes of another outcome?"

"I did. They weren't great hopes. I was worried. We have friends who said, 'We're going to win,' but as the evening wore on my heart sank deeper and deeper and deeper. The next morning I really felt like someone had kicked me. And it was Terrence's birthday. I had a speaking engagement upstate in Glen Falls to a group of people with HIV. I was leaving him on his birthday with Bush in the presidency. I had this five-hour lonely drive. It was terrible."

I've laid out a platter of Scottish smoked salmon and Murray's bagels on my coffee table but Tom refuses my offer of food. I ask if he wants coffee and, if so, regular coffee or espresso.

"Okay, an espresso," he reluctantly replies.

Though I've been dying for a bagel, I make us each a cup of Italian espresso, but leave the bagels untouched. We discuss the bulk e-mail that's been making the rounds:

The Democrats' mistake was in thinking that a disastrous war and national bankruptcy would be of concern to the electorate.

The Republicans correctly saw that the chief concern of the electorate was to keep gay couples from having an abortion.

It makes me laugh but Tom shakes his head sorrowfully.

"It's too true to laugh at."

"Was there anyone in your childhood who inspired you to be of use?" I ask.

"A number of them. I call my parents soup kitchen Catholics. There was a lot about feeding the poor, housing the homeless, loving thy neighbor. I got that message from both of my folks. Two books influenced me, altered my life, *To Kill a Mockingbird* was one. Atticus had this great sense of justice and risk-taking. When I think about it, I think Scout probably grew up to be a lesbian. The other book was *The Diary of Anne Frank*. At a very young age I knew I identified with Anne Frank in some way. I probably read her diary ten times. Without being crass about it, and I never never never want to lessen people's horrific struggles, but as a young person closeted I felt a kinship with her. I felt so hidden."

"Imprisoned?"

"Imprisoned. I had all these dreams. My life was an interior life. I didn't feel I could share these dreams, I felt this psychological imprisonment. I've gotten over that but I still keep Anne's diary close by my bed."

"Were you in a long-term relationship before?"

"I was in a seven-year relationship in my twenties. We lived together."

Tom is slim and agile, with soulful eyes, an open face, and close-cropped hair.

"And have you found love different now that you're a lot older?"

"It's less hysterical. It's a lot more confident. I don't want to say it's better because I don't want to dishonor Pete but . . . I think I'm more ready for it. It's much richer. I've accepted that I'm lovable. I am aware of my own mortality now."

"Do you feel that we love for different reasons when we're older? Or what we want is different?"

Tom pauses to consider my question. "Hmmm. No. I think we love because we want to be loved and have so much love to give. I think our awareness may evolve."

"Do you expect more?"

"No. It's just more glorious. I don't think love is possessive. I sort of want to be surprised every day, and three years into it, that has been the case."

"Do you think you would have been attracted to Terrence when you were twenty?"

"Definitely."

"It defies all chronology?"

"I have to say I was probably OCD about him but I was obsessive about parsing out the celebrity from the person."

"How did you do that?"

"You make sure that most of your dates are just the two of you; that they are not about going to openings. Make sure he meets some of your friends. . . ."

"Did anyone help you with this?"

"It was my own personal logic. I think that"—he wells up—"he saw I was attracted to *him*. It was amazing, it was electric."

"How do you feel about aging? Are you frightened?"

Tom dabs at his eyes with the side of his hand. "I'm not frightened."

"What about physical changes?"

"It mostly makes me laugh 'cause I feel it. I got a haircut recently. Some of it . . . most of it was gray. There's a hair here"—he points to the back—"a hair here."

He points to his cheek.

"You mean a stray strand?"

"Yeah."

"Do men get that too?"

"Oh, yeah. You ask yourself, Where did this come from? I have to get out of my car like this."

He stands in a crouched position.

"Oh, come on."

"Oh, yeah. When I exercise, when I'm in shape, I'm like a little VW Beetle. But even in a station wagon, I can't just jump out. I don't think about my age a lot be-

Tom and Terrence

cause I'm so blessed. I'm HIV negative. I think about mortality all the time and it's not my own. I *am* mindful that my spouse has a Medicare card."

"And a senior transit card."

"He loves that. He jokes about it all the time. But I am mindful. In the natural order of things it is likely that he'll predecease me. There are moments when that scares me."

He tears up again.

"But love is love. We really celebrate life."

I ask about his wedding.

"My wedding was probably the happiest day of my life."

"What did you wear?"

"We wore red sweaters. Red's the color of love. They weren't the same, just red sweaters. It was in Vermont. It was in front of a fireplace. We brought our dog up with us, a little Yorkshire terrier. We drove Terrence's car that is nicer than mine to West Dover, Vermont. We have friends who'd stayed at this inn and who used this justice of the peace. I really wanted to be married by a woman. We contacted Millicent, who is an assessor for the town of West Dover. She was lovely. So perfect. She wore a very holiday festive kind of outfit with poinsettias."

"How was she qualified as a justice of the peace?"

"She was elected. We exchanged our vows. We did it on Friday night, December twentieth."

"Winter solstice."

"Yes."

"The shortest day of the year."

"It was really wonderful, just great. It was so otherworldly . . . like having an out-of-body experience because all of a sudden this government official came to the inn and said these words we'd heard all our lives."

"The traditional?"

"Yes. Till death do you part. In sickness and in health. We exchanged rings."

"Did you get a certificate?"

"Yes. A license."

I ask if it had been written up anywhere.

"There was a traditional announcement in the *New York Times*. But we didn't get the biggest that Sunday, that went to Senator John Warner, one of Elizabeth Taylor's exes."

Terrence McNally, Thomas Kirdahy

Terrence McNally, *the playwright, and Thomas Joseph Kir-*
dahy, a public-interest lawyer, affirmed their partnership last
evening at the Inn at Sawmill Farm in West Dover, VT. Milli-
cent B. Atkins, a justice of the peace for Dover, VT, performed
the civil union ceremony.

Mr. McNally, 65, *won Tony awards for best play for* Love!
Valour! Compassion! *(1995) and* Master Class *(1996) and*
for the best book of a musical for his adaptation of Kiss of the
Spider Woman *(1993) and* Frankie and Johnny in the Clair
de Lune *(1987) and* Lips Together, Teeth Apart *(1991)* . . .

Mr. Kirdahy, 40, *is a public advocate in Riverhead, NY, with*
Nassau-Suffolk Law Services, a nonprofit program that provides
legal assistance in civil matters to low-income clients. He special-
izes in representing people with HIV or AIDS. . . .

The couple met at Guild Hall in East Hampton, NY, in the
summer of 2001 when Mr. Kirdahy, who was then the chairman
of the East End Gay Organization of Long Island, organized
a panel discussion called "Fear from a Gay Perspective." The
panel included Mr. McNally, Edward Albee and Langford
Wilson.

"I met him backstage at Guild Hall, in the wings," Mr. Mc-
Nally recalled, noting that he quickly took to Mr. Kirdahy. But
Mr. McNally was leaving the next day for a long trip to Peru and
agreed to look him up when he got back. "We became a couple
fairly soon after," Mr. McNally said. . . .

"And September 11 happened, and my mother died."

After that, his relationship with Mr. Kirdahy became a much
closer one. "When you've lost so much, you tend to cut to the
chase quickly," Mr. McNally said. . . .

"The name of the panel was actually 'Theater from a Gay Perspective' and not 'Fear,' as it appears," Tom tells me.

"If there was a movie about you and Terrence, who would you like to see play the parts?"

He doesn't answer right away. Finally he does: "My friends at work have always said Tom Hanks should play me because of his mix of goofiness and seriousness. I think I agree with them. An understudy would be Robert Downey, Jr. Terrence would be played by Paul Newman because of his great good looks and the kindness in his eyes."

When Tom leaves, I slice a bagel in half, slather cream cheese and lox onto one of the halves and take a big bite. It's a cold bright day, and the sky is azure blue. When I go back to the sitting area I notice that he didn't drink his espresso. I wonder why. I hope it was drinkable.

"When I met him I was bold"

Because he's so busy, and unless I'm willing to wait for two months—which I'm not—it's necessary to interview Terrence by telephone:

"I've been very busy."

"Is there any particular new work?" I ask him.

"I've just got a lot of projects at different stages of development. I'm busier than I've ever been. It's taken me . . . I've been back on the track . . . for about a year now. I realize that cancer surgery was major. It took a good two years out of my life. I thought the minute the pain of the surgery was over, I could just bounce back. It didn't work that way. Tom and I hadn't had many dates when I found out that I had the cancer. We certainly weren't committed partners. I remember him saying to me when I told him I had to have surgery, 'I will be there for you if you would like that.' He did not say, 'I'll be there for you.' I thought it was so classy for him to say, '*if* you'd like it,' not jumping into your life, no grandstand heroics."

"Do you and Tom have a favorite love song?"

"Yes. 'Always.'"

"'Always.' Wow."

"Simple Irving Berlin. No complications. Very direct melody, lyric."

"If there was a movie or a play about yours and Tom's life, who would you cast to play yourself?"

"I would cast Tom Hanks to play me. I'm trying to think of contemporary people. I just love Tom Hanks. He has a big heart. He's not worried about being a movie star, he embraces humanity. I'd be happy to be seen that way."

"And who would play Tom?"

"Oh God. . . . Tim Robbins will be Tom."

"Oh great."

"Somebody with a real social . . ."

"That's pretty sexy."

". . . conscience. And sexy too. A real doer. Not insulated. I like people who are in the real world, not just isolated in their own ego."

"You know the F. Scott Fitzgerald quote: 'There are no second acts in American lives.'"

"Yeah."

"Any comments on that."

"It was not true in my life. We all have a good first act. Ha, ha. Some people have a second. I would say my life's had three acts. Maybe four. Right now is my third. Being sick was a demarcation point. It was three years ago this week that I had the surgery. The first of two. It's very easy to define my life in three acts."

"Do you know the Oscar Wilde quote that said, 'A second marriage is a triumph of hope over experience'?"

"No."

"Any comment?"

"Triumph *over* experience? I've been in more than one significant relationship. I experienced a loss. My last lover Gary died of AIDS."

I hadn't known this.

"Gary! That was a very fulfilling relationship. I was very happy in it. When it ended, I didn't expect it to happen. If I'm understanding Oscar Wilde, it sounds like he's saying that good relationships are impossible, good marriages are impossible. I don't believe it. I think you have to be mature to be a good partner to someone. I think that's one reason we have such a high divorce rate, straight or gay, in this country, because when people get committed or married in their early twenties it seems they are just asking for disaster. I certainly didn't know very much at that age . . . someone who was drinking . . . a little crazy too."

There's some kind of cacophony of car horns down below.

"So much of my relationship with the world is much different than when I was drinking. That's another demarcation point in my life. My first two long-term relationships . . . I've really had five . . . the first two were completely involved with people who drank as much as I did. In a funny way I almost don't count them. That was the end of act one. And then I got sober."

"What year?"

"It's going to be twenty-four years. When I was getting sober the relationship I was in floundered. I think he maybe had enough of living with an active alcoholic. I've been a one-hundred-percent sober person with Gary and Tom. Tom's sober too, you know. It makes me sound like Elizabeth Taylor. My relationships were all long-term ones, more than five or six years, so you have to count them. They're not dalliances by any means. I think maturity is what I mean by experience. It's so much a part of my relationship with Tom. I bring a good experience to it. A lot of experience."

"Do you think getting older and having a near-death experience, as you did, renders the pleasure in loving and being loved and sexuality keener?"

"I think it did in my case. I've been very happy in my life. I was very happy with Gary without the drama of the cancer. With Tom it's so much a part of our story. I know people say things like, 'Cancer's the best thing that ever happened to me.' I don't want to make a remark like that but yes, I've been more sensitive to people and my mortality. I was with Gary when he died, but it took my own cancer for me to recognize my own mortality, that I will be the person who's going this time. Certainly the cancer has made me enjoy everything more keenly. Gary and Tom are both such amazing men. They brought their own keenness and appreciation with them. You don't know Gary. It's funny, I really think Gary sent Tom to me. It's wonderful that I can talk about Gary with Tom when I feel a need to. He's not at all threatened by it. Most relationships end through breakup. Mutual. One that ends sadly through one passing is a very different experience."

"Do you feel guilty loving and feeling happy at a time of so much misery in the world?"

"Sometimes you do feel almost selfish when you're very happy. I have a lot of friends who are single who are my age, who didn't find love again after their thirties or forties. I have a couple of friends to my knowledge they've never been in a really intense, loving relationship. Sometimes when I'm with them I censor myself a little bit about how happy Tom and I are. I said to him one night, 'Do you feel we're physically different with one another around certain people?' He said, 'Yes.' You don't want to rub it in. Just, for lack of a better word, flaunting our intimacy at someone else who doesn't have it. Guilt? It's more sadness than anything. I think people give up. I really do. That's why I wrote my play *Frankie and Johnny* because I had turned forty . . . I mean fifty. I became very aware as a single man in New York City how many men my age and younger were . . ."

He pauses, then continues, "I'd see them in the video store renting six movies and they'd have their Häagen-Dazs and that's how they are planning to spend the weekend."

"Do you have any words of hope?"

"I think you have to put yourself out there. I think dating, once you're beyond high school, is very humiliating and you just have to suffer the indignation of it. I've had blind dates where the minute the door opened, you're furious at your friends thinking you could possibly like the person. Or, one person I thought was quite attractive, at the end of the evening he said, 'I could never be interested in you that way.' I was fifty-one years old. I suddenly felt I was back at Ray High School in Corpus Christi, Texas, when you're told, 'Oh, I don't like you. I don't want to kiss you.'"

We laugh.

"It's very hard for an adult to date. I think it's an adolescent experience. All I'm saying is I think you've got to keep trying. It's so easy to shut down. The way we live now with e-mail and DVD and answering machines, cell phones, we can just put up a smoke screen of indifference, of being busy all the time. You've got to get out where other people are, single people. I met Tom because I said yes to a silly panel on gay theater. Not that the panel itself was silly but I thought all such panels were silly. But, I did not go to that evening thinking I was going to meet Tom. When I met him I was bold. I'm twenty-five years older than Tom but I said, I'd like to see you again. That takes a certain amount of *chutzpah* . . . guts. Thank God he said okay. Even though he had apprehensions about it too, one because I'm, quote, better known than he is, I'm in the public eye. He didn't know if I was sober. From my work he probably thought I was a big hellraiser. He had his foreboding. But he was brave too and took a second step."

He sighs.

"We really enjoy each other enormously. I don't know how to put it. It's a miracle! In the space of three months Terrence is going to have lung cancer, his mother is going to die and 9/11 is going to happen. Any one of those would have been a lot. By the way, a month ago they told me they consider me cancer free. They said, 'We consider you one of the miracle people.' I'm glad I didn't know how bad the statistics were for lung cancer when I had the surgery. And sometimes—I think I told you—I think Gary's spirit sent Tom. Almost the same day I met Tom his sister, Gary's sister, who's about forty . . . a man came up to her in a parking lot and said, 'I'd love to buy you a cup of coffee.' And she said, 'I'm not used to having men hit on me.' And they've been living together ever since."

"Gary was busy."

"Gary was really working. But you have to put yourself out there and get your heart stepped on a little bit. You have to be bold. We're planning to celebrate our anniversary. We've been together three years. Sounds quick . . . short. Let's hope we can get twenty out of it. Who knows."

"Happy anniversary!"

Libido

I've been taken to lunch at a Szechuan restaurant in Connecticut by the publicist and the organizer of a book event at which I've just participated. I can't help but ogle a bluish, pinkish tattoo that resembles morning glories decorating the forearm of the publicist. When she lifts the metallic pot to pour tea, I see that the flowers are attached to a leafy vine that coils round her arm. A platter of crabmeat dumplings are quickly deposited on the table. The organizer and the publicist, both women in midlife, seem to be old friends. Very quickly they forget me, forget my book.

The publicist says to the organizer, "I heard you've been dating Simon Kimmel. You may not know it but Simon and I went to high school together. Are you sleeping together?"

I don't know Simon Kimmel, but I'm curious too.

"Funny you should mention sex," the organizer replies, "because last night we finally got around to talking about whether or not things could really work out for us. Simon and I discussed finances, living arrangements, snoring and so on. Finally Simon decided it was time to broach the subject of sex for the first time."

"Oh!"

Rice and garlicky spinach are brought to the table by the waitress.

The organizer continues, "'We're not spring chickens any-more,' Simon announced to me as if I don't know. 'I was wondering how you feel about sex,' he continued bravely. 'Well,' I said, responding very carefully, knowing Simon is very literal-minded, 'I have to say that I will like it infrequently.' Simon brooded quietly for a moment, then looked at me over his bifocals, and asked, 'Was that one word or two?'"

Later, while driving my rental car, I ponder why the subject of sex is such a source of seriousness and merriment, one and the same.

"I've begun enjoying penetrative sex"

I've pulled several clippings from my file folder to show the woman I'm about to interview at my apartment. One's a wedding announcement in the *New York Times*. The bride, Elaine Schecter, an anthropologist and writer, was fifty-three and the groom, David Herscher, a publicist, fifty-seven. Theirs was a June wedding:

> . . . *[the couple] met through a personal advertisement Mr. Herscher placed in a Manhattan neighborhood newspaper. Ms. Schecter had circled the ad week after week but just did not get around to answering it. One week it was no longer there.*

"What occurred to me is, they'll close down his voice mail and he will disappear into a black hole in the cosmos, and I will never find him," she said. "There was this almost irresistible nagging intuition saying, 'If you don't respond to this ad, you're going to regret it.' I had to scramble through a pile of old newspapers to find it."

Mr. Herscher, having received responses from 80 women and having gone on dates with 20 of them, had canceled the ad. He had found the women who responded varied and interesting and yet not just right. Still, weeks after the ad stopped running, he dialed in to check for a new response.

"I said, 'This is absolutely the last time I'm calling,' and it said, 'You have one new message,'" he remembered. *"The one new message was Elaine."*

The woman I'm about to interview is the one my friend Barbara had suggested I speak with. On the phone she'd mentioned that she'd answered ads in her search for a partner. When she arrives, I serve her orange juice at my glass dining table. She is a tall, voluptuous blonde, with the whitest teeth I've ever seen and a snub nose. I show her the Schecter/Herscher announcement.

"The ads I answered were raunchy from the get-go. You see, I was into sex, not romance, at that point."

Beatrix White lives and works in Detroit but has come to New York to attend a conference. She's forty-seven, is wearing silver earrings that dangle. Before I go into the kitchen to make our omelets, I read her a few statistics from one of my clippings, a survey done by Durex, the condom manufacturer. "According to a sex survey, people around the world spend an average 19.7 minutes on foreplay. Britons spend the most time on foreplay—22.5 minutes—and

Thais the least, only 11.5 minutes. It says that the younger age groups take the longest to warm up—between 19.1 and 21.6 minutes. But people in middle age spend only 17.3 minutes on foreplay. Care to comment?"

Her laughter has a ribald edge to it.

"That's interesting. It does take me less time to warm up these days . . . but I hadn't thought about it in minutes or seconds. Does it mention Argentineans?"

I'd pretty well briefed her on the telephone about what I wanted to talk about, so she gets right down to it with no small talk.

"I've been thinking about what it is . . . the second act . . . how do I fit into that."

She follows me to the kitchen, sipping from her coffee cup. She leans against the door frame of my tiny kitchen, while I crack open fresh eggs.

"For women, the big thing is, is it pre-childbearing or post? For me, the new relationship I started recently is post-childbearing. Absolutely and unequivocally because I had a hysterectomy last year. I think what's really interesting about my new relationship is that this is the first time I've actually begun to enjoy penetrative sex . . . at age forty-seven. Part of that is I no longer have to worry about pregnancy. We've had HIV tests. No more bloody awful periods taking up a part of every month. Sex is very different because of that. And I know about sex. I've spent years studying it."

Beatrix was born in Brighton, England, where her father worked in a factory and her mother stayed home, growing roses. Her father moved the family to Detroit in the 1980s where he opened a nursery and greenhouse. Beatrix became a veterinarian and has a practice in Detroit. She still speaks with a glib English accent.

"I'm finding sex more and more exciting. I really couldn't optimally enjoy penetrative sex for my whole life. I was more clitoral than vaginal. But now I'm with someone who's open about these things. It's like the beginning of a journey. I think one of these days I might have an orgasm."

There's a wicked edge to her laughter.

"Were you an orgasm faker?"

"No. I never faked. I've only faked an orgasm on the telephone, just to get it over with."

"Phone sex! So you've really explored . . ."

"God, yes. Of course I've always been involved in politics. In the seventies and eighties we of course had penetrative sex. But . . . God . . . it stood for what oppressed women."

"How?"

"There was the notion that men were imposing themselves, raping women. They had to pay, being men."

In her middle thirties Bea decided she was going to have a child on her own. She researched artificial insemination, found out where she could get it. Had to see a counselor. Then she investigated artificial insemination from sperm donors.

"The way it works, you choose your little bit of information on your donor . . . what they look like and so on. They're mostly medical students. Then you have to lie down and the doctor puts a turkey baster–type thing deep inside. You have to lie there with your legs up, then you drive home and wait to see if you're pregnant. When you're not, you pay your money and go again."

I flip our omelet, hand Bea the cloth napkins.

"I did it nine different times when I was ovulating. But I kept on not getting pregnant. Each month I'd think, I'm pregnant. I'm pregnant. But I wasn't. Then you come to a point where the doctor says, 'Look. It's not happening. There are problems. The only thing to do is get a laparoscopy.' Of course, at this point all my friends are having children."

Finally she stopped trying after reluctantly deciding that she simply wasn't going to get pregnant.

"I'd had so much sex, so many affairs, so many one-night stands in my life, I finally realized that not a single man in the world would be right for me. This is when my dad died. My dad's a working-class man. That's the kind of man I always liked. As I got older I liked a 'bit of rough' as we say."

After forty she began dating through classified newspaper ads. Of course she only used classifieds from the left-wing newspaper.

"I had my perimeters."

She stops talking while the warbling wail of a siren goes by. Before we can resume our conversation, the ear-piercing clack of fire trucks intrudes. Bea helps to carry our breakfast to the table.

"Between males with sick dogs in the back of their pickups and the classifieds, I met lots of men. But, what would usually happen would be I'd meet someone who was awfully nice but we'd have no sexual chemistry at all. I didn't want any more friends, I had loads of friends."

One of the ads she answered was an Argentinean guy whom she didn't meet for quite some time.

"We started on the telephone. He's in Hawaii, he's an architect. We start having telephone sex. And, when we did meet, I felt a bit—Oh God—but I'm too far into this. I didn't know such a thing existed but he's a sex addict, obsessed with sex. He uses prostitutes, spends all his time thinking about it. He told me that once he got chicken pox and lost his libido and it was just an incredible relief."

The omelet is undercooked.

"Actually I much preferred him on the phone than in person.

He was ten years younger. He was a bit creepy. But what happened with this guy was that—finally, at an older age—I started to get into sex. The thing about telephone sex is that you talk about things a lot because that's all you're doing. I didn't like him, didn't want any contact with him but he did me an enormous favor in that he opened me up sexually. I was now in my early forties. He was a stepping-stone."

In 1999, Beatrix was forty-two. Because her career was booming, she decided to enlarge her office, then she bought a condo. At the same time, she started learning Spanish and went to Argentina on a holiday.

"I had the most fantastic time in Buenos Aires. So I decided, what the hell, I went back home and took a leave of absence. Then I went back to Buenos Aires for three months of painting watercolors, speaking Spanish, dating hot Argentineans. That liberated me in some way. I am a different person in Argentina than I am in America. Before I was this spiky, prickly person. I couldn't be clever in the new language, so I was treated differently by people."

I dash back into the kitchen for pepper and salt.

"In my second act I started becoming another person. Completely. I changed massively. I started becoming just a happier person. This began at a time when I was earning my money in Detroit but just living to go back to Buenos Aires. In Buenos Aires I'm fifty percent better looking than I am in Michigan—tall, blond. Tall is great there. Sex is different. The men I'd been with at home . . . they've been crippled by liberated women in a way. The men back home are terrified of me."

The Argentine thing lasted awhile. Finally it wore thin. She woke up one morning and decided that she wanted a sustaining, grown-up relationship.

"Suddenly my favorite aunt died of cancer and then I had to have a hysterectomy. After the surgery, I stayed with my mother and cried all the time because it's certain now that I'll never have a child."

On Halloween she went to a party and got pretty drunk. Bea and some of her friends decided to go to a second party.

"We trooped down the hill. It had just begun to snow. I walked into the gathering and looked around to see whom I'm going to flirt with. I see this guy. Someone says he's a businessman. He's standing on his own. He later told me he knew who I was because he's brought his cockatiel in to see me. I didn't remember. I was quite aggressive, I remember. I said, 'Surprise me.' He says, 'I'm a widower.' I said, 'Oh, you have surprised me.' I decided to go back to the other party. Outside the snow was sticking. It's slippery snow. I'm wearing high heels. This guy, Mark, sees me heading out and I plop on my ass. He offers to accompany me. We snark as snow falls."

"Snark?"

"Kiss."

Bea describes how she went back to the party and didn't think anything of it. Almost to the hour on the anniversary of her father's death, Mark telephoned and asked her out.

"I'm in bed. I think, What a nice voice he has. So we go out and I audition him for two weeks. On the first date I liked his jacket, but . . . Oh my God . . . the shoes. They looked like something you'd wear to a wedding in the eighties. He's got the slight air of a man who's been on his own too long."

Her plate is empty.

"Second date. The shoes come out again. Again I'm thinking, Those revolting shoes! How superficial are you? I don't fancy him.

He's not someone I fancy; though I know he fancies me. You see, he's really posh. He's been to a private school . . . comes from money. But I go out with him again anyway. I'm in my pre-holiday dry-out. So while we're going out, I'm not drinking. I've always drunk and had sex quickly. In my mind being posh means being a screw-up but I start to like him."

They get on well, talk on the telephone a lot. Then Bea had to go out of town. When she came back there was an enormous bunch of flowers awaiting from Mark.

"When I next talked to him on the telephone, he said, 'How about if I come to your house for the weekend?' Funny, that's exactly what I was going to do, invite him."

A sexual relationship began.

"It's absolutely clear that this is the really big relationship."

"So you're compatible sexually?"

"Yeah. It's new. We're sexually very active and loving. We're very similar about sex. It doesn't faze him at all that I've had lots of lovers, that my body is . . . well, less springy. Sex just becomes more and more better for me."

"The hysterectomy didn't change you sexually?"

"Slightly. The intensity of the orgasm is a bit dulled but on the other hand, not having horrific bleeding, period pains, not having to worry about contraceptives. Didn't I see pastries in the kitchen?"

Bea and Mark decided to do the HIV test. They shocked each other when they decided to commit to monogamy.

"I've never done this before. I completely trust this man. It's a fantastic revelation. True, I'm sexually still attracted to others but I want an enduring relationship. I've made a decision. That's what it is. I really want this. I want it to work."

"I was glad to know my equipment still worked"

Paula Thornber is a violinist who lives in Soho and plays with a small string quartet. She was widowed when she was forty-seven. Her husband Misha, also a violinist, had been diagnosed with cancer, then died two years later. She's been a widow for eight years and has a grown daughter who's a social worker in Atlanta. I meet her at the corner of Mott and Canal. She'd told me on the phone that she was having an affair, her first in years. We begin walking west toward the subway. She's a big-boned woman, who wears designer glasses and speaks like a Bryn Mawr instructor, though with surprising sprinklings of vulgarity.

"When I heard myself referring to my twenties and thirties as something in the distant past, it was the first time I realized that my youth was truly gone. Gone forever. I felt like I was in no-man's-land. I had no map."

We walk along Canal Street crowded with Chinese selling food and vegetables from stands. A group of young children carrying balloons and wearing party hats pass us.

I ask with whom she's having this new affair.

"A rather unlikely man, a surgeon named Ed. I was fixed up with him by—of all people—my dentist. We had an awkward blind date. I didn't really feel like seeing him again, but I thought I shouldn't make a decision too quickly. He invited me for a walk across the Brooklyn Bridge on a Friday night. I was off, so I said yes."

She describes how the awkwardness of their first date dissipated very quickly when they reached the center of the bridge.

"It was near sunset, the city was aglow, and by the time we

reached Manhattan, he was holding my hand. My heart was pounding. Can you believe it? I'm middle-aged and my heart is pounding like a thirteen-year-old! We walked right to his apartment in Murray Hill and went to bed."

"Your libido?"

"Despite lack of use, and a painful cramp in the back of my neck midway, I was glad to know that my equipment still worked. The next morning in bed after a breakfast of croissants and Danish butter we had a lusty erotic reprise; then we decided to spend the weekend together and began the day by taking a taxi up to the Metropolitan Museum."

There are brackish pools of water at every corner left by last night's rain.

"That was about ten days ago and—candidly—my v hasn't stopped tingling yet."

We reach the entrance to the Eighth Avenue subway. She promises to keep me apprised.

"That is, if I hear from him again."

S he doesn't call for a while but when she does, she invites me to meet her at the Metropolitan Museum of Art for a drink. When I see her waiting at the restaurant, she gives me a bright smile.

"My erotic engine is now in third gear."

"Oh!"

"Since their reemergence, I've been experiencing extraordinarily strong—almost unbearable—erotic feelings."

She calls the waiter and orders a martini.

"An orgasm may only be a rush of oxytocin and vasopressin, but it packs quite a wallop."

Of what? I don't comment, just beg, "Wait! Go back to where you left me on Canal Street. You'd just spent the weekend with this surgeon. You'd just restarted your libido."

She giggles.

"Yes. That's true. Well, when it became an actual affair, I decided to keep a diary. When my heart and legs began to open, the feelings were so poignant that I felt the need to record everything. I promised I'd keep you apprised. Here."

She removes a notebook speckled in black and white from her black vinyl Channel 13 carryall and hands it to me.

"I think this will give you an idea of how we're doing better than I can in conversation. I've marked excerpts 'FYI' that relate to Ed and me. It begins after that first *schtupp*."

We finish our drinks and she leaves for a rehearsal. Since I have time, I walk through the antiquities, then take the subway home. That night I take her notebook into bed with me.

FYI: September 3rd: After Ed and I left the museum, I steered us into Central Park. We walked around the sailboat pond. It was a perfect afternoon, the fine light washing across water and grass and trees. I felt my cynical heart go soft, felt waves of piquant, garden-variety lust lapping from vaginal lips to fingertips. Would you like to sit down, Ed? I asked, motioning toward an empty park bench. No, he replied, taking my arm, bringing the frame of his sixty-three-year-old body alongside, in contact with, mine.

He plucked my hand as one would who was pulling a weed and we accelerated the pace of our walk which took us downtown through the zoo past the Plaza Hotel, through afternoon crowds of tourists at Rockefeller Center, through changing light. A fresh moistness infused the air. He disregarded red lights on Fifth Av-

enue, walked between honking trucks and cabs. I could tell he
was a bit of an outlaw. When we got to Murray Hill, he took me
home to his sleigh bed and once again—AND HOW—took my
breath away.

We walked seventy blocks together that day.

The markings stop there. Below are comments about a phone
call with her daughter and some kind of list and more, so I scan
down to the next FYI:

FYI: September 9th: We made love and love and love and love
and love last night. We twisted and spun like kites/tops/gyroscopes/
gymnasts/skydivers. We lay together, glommed around each other
in a perfect, exhausted, satiated, post-orgasmic fit, like a bottle
finding its top, a fitted sheet peeled over its right-sized mattress.

The day ended, another began with more lovemaking. Bright
blood spotted the very white sheet; bruised fingerprints remained
on my arms for a week. A pulse close to delirium fibrillated, still
fibrillates, in my neck.

Should I tell Ed I love you? Am I falling in love? Is Misha
turning over in his grave?

FYI: Sept. 12th: He ordered a delivery of Chinese food that we
ate in bed. We didn't speak, needed nothing. My Chinese fortune
cookie said: "Your heart will always make itself known through
your words." My lucky numbers were 2, 6, 16, 29, 30 and 41.

He gave me a key to his apartment.

I still haven't said the words "I love you." Why? I would have
done so when I was twenty.

FYI: September 17th: I waited for him in his apartment,
wearing black silk pajamas. His flight was arriving at 9:14 in the

*evening; a car was waiting to bring him home. I'd put fresh white
tulips into an Italian ceramic vase on top of his wardrobe, a black
bottle of German love oil on his white pillowcase and a sexy Nina
Simone CD into the player. While I waited, I listened to every
salty word, then played another CD—Jacqueline du Pré's heart-
sick cello; passing the time.*

*His world is white on white; his duvet cover, sheets, robe,
monogrammed pajamas, towels are white. His walls are a museum
of various half-kitsch nature-scapes, a Klee drawing and wall-to-
ceiling shelves engorged with books about the brain and Buddhism.
I thought about his hands and feet, their sometimes coolness against
my hot skin. I conjured the delineation of his ribs when I embrace
him, how his nipples, like Cupid's arrows, sear mine.*

*When I heard his key in the door, I leaped up to greet him,
wanted to cry with . . . with what? Happiness maybe. The nub
of that joy remained/remains unsaid, unnamed, though that
moist nub did slide between my lips and legs.*

*Once again I didn't say I love you. When I brought it up in
analysis, asked Dr. K. what she thought, her answer was the
usual silence.*

*FYI: Sept. 21st: Ed and I share: Acts of love. A cocoon of
love. A loving atmosphere. Moments of loving kindness. A hundred forms of lovemaking. Concentric, radiating beeps of strong
feeling. Love of books. We don't share any words of love or en-
dearment.*

*FYI: Sept. 26th: My heart rose up like a phoenix at the sight
of Ed's face coming toward me through the face-filled lobby of his
downtown hospital. Above me, outside, a dazzling sliver of new
moon to bring us luck. I called out to him and, hearing his name,
he hastened his step, descended four marble steps, gripped and*

squeezed my arm, fondled my buttocks. I called him darling, an-
gel, muse. An ache of . . . (of what?) . . . bled through my wool
dress, an arrow to the groin, caused my knees to weaken.

FYI: October 3rd: I came out of the shower in gold silk paja-
mas. He was across the room, ramrod straight, head bowed, eyes
closed, on his meditation cushion. He wore a sweater in a soft
fabric that made my fingertips tingle—pale gray wool mixed with
confetti of white. The unsaid foamed internally in a torrent, it
floated up in white froth, in visceral waterfall. It pounded and
poured against the sharp edges of my shopworn heart.

Unsaid but experienced with such tender permeation, I mind-
fully bit down on and burst the grape of loving Ed.

The next morning, I drop the notebook back into its envelope
and leave it with her doorman. A few weeks later, Paula and I have
lunch at a French place in the meatpacking district. She gives me
another set of FYI entries.

FYI: October 18th: Before I left the bedroom Ed was reading the
Wall Street Journal in his unrumpled bed. (How does he do it?
Sleep all night between covers and sheets and wake as if the bed
was still made.) I made and poured coffee for myself in his sun-
less kitchen. Then I sat in the library and reconstituted the swatch
of days we'd just spent together:

I remembered the high note he'd sounded on the Friday before
the weekend when he started an e-mail to me with the words "my
darling," how it had quenched a thirst, cracked the door of affec-
tionate language we'd never opened before. I'd held his words in
my hand like a lucky coin all day, until we met in his bed at 11,
both of us returned from our separate evenings, and tentatively,

after bare bones of conviviality, brought our naked bodies together on newly washed and ironed white sheets.

He was tired, I had sprained my ankle. Nevertheless, the
faucet of desire turned; a trickle dribbled, then a stream gushed,
releasing a forceful outpouring of pleasure and intimacy that
flooded my being with his being; that overflowed from a bountiful
source. Our lips joined. He was so beloved to me at that moment
that fissures of tenderness opened in my heart. None of this less-
ened or abated, but remained at full throttle, when we finally
turned, Ed one way, me the other, as Mother Nature brought
down the curtain of sleep.

FYI: We slept late on Saturday. I felt scrubbed clean with a
cloth of fragrant happiness and good fortune, with Virginia
Woolf's "a free day a perfect pearl" ahead. Ed leaned over and
kissed my cheek, his (always) cool hand swiped my arm. His fingers entangled with mine and our lips brushed. Then, as his time
for activity had come, our sensual closeness dropped away like a
glass swept from a table and smashed by a careless hand.

On Saturday and Sunday we irritated each other. He criti-
cized me because I'd left the top off the toothpaste tube. I couldn't
believe it, but he did. Later he angrily showed me a kitchen cabinet I'd forgotten to shut, filling me with shame. He had actually
chastised me, as if I was a six-year-old. I made no defense,
couldn't break out of my lumpish passivity, was tongue-tied. I became monosyllabic, moody, joyless because he'd incited me to
hurt and anger with his tendency toward obsessive-compulsive
ways. I was restless. I walked around on eggs. He was cool, distant, did his bills, talked on the phone, read, silently quartered his
orange in a way that had begun to annoy me. I went over the new
score, didn't breathe.

Neither of us engaged, while the kitchen clock ticked, car horns bleeped repeatedly. We slept side by side for two more nights. Our tongues didn't meet, mingle or mix but our feet and backs and bottoms met, pressed softlysoftly as the wind blew the curtain into the darkened room, making it dance.

When he went off to a daylong Buddhist retreat in Tribeca, tears welled. They dried and left an emptiness so acidic it burnt. I met him for an Italian lunch during his break. He asked me the questions the leader had asked at the retreat: "What do you plan to do with your one wild and precious life? What makes you come alive?"

I went back to his apartment. I thought about time we'd spent together, a tossed salad of darks and lights, a soup as tart as it is sweet. I was asleep when he came home and slept through the night. I woke to the sound of him on his treadmill, Good Morning America *blaring from the TV. I wanted to enfold him in my arms, have all be right/clean/easy/sexy with us. I wanted to tear out the acrimony from my heart; wanted only sweetness, lightness; wanted him to love and treasure me; wanted to love and cherish him. What will I, a widow, do with this wild and precious, Pandora's box of love? What will it do with me?*

Not to intrude on his treadmill exercise, I said good-bye from the doorway. Breathing in and out, in and out, inandout I tossed the coin of "my darling" high up into the air, caught it in my palm, and walked into the street. As we'd slept, the curtain of autumn had lifted to reveal the first inkling of winter complete with snow flurries, frost, the fresh cologne of mystery and hope in the air.

I'm sorry that Paula's new affair is faltering. When next I hear from her, she's gone off to Puerto Rico, but has left the same manila envelope with her doorman.

FYI: November 4th: He gave me my walking papers while sitting on his gold couch with his two long legs stretched out before him.

A squeeze of sadness passes through my heart. I realize I've been rooting for Paula and Ed. I read on:

His face was an unreadable, angry mask; his words were spoken in a cold, measured, executive tone; a tone I guessed he uses at the hospital to fire no-longer-wanted employees. We both knew that the glass of our affair with the lovely ring was shattered. He had the courage to say Basta while I waited for one last . . . One last what? Walk around the park? Cool hand on a hot breast? A last dance after the music had stopped?

I left his building at 10:30 that night. I left with my heart clenched, my eyes burning, went home in a smelly taxi and began refinishing my antique desk.

Day 1: Felt cut up and drained all day but also as if a fever or delirium had lifted.

Day 2: Felt liberated and elated all day. Fever free.

Day 3: Experienced bursts of anger, dips of sadness, made a mental laundry list that disparaged him, momentarily couldn't re-member what I had loved, realized that trying to fit into his rigid, contained life had been as contortionist for me as a Houdini trick.

Day 4: The temperature dropped to 10 below. I practiced none-theless, experienced near euphoria when the big insurance check from Misha's estate arrived in the mail.

FYI: November 9th: When I walked to meet Rita for dinner, the white-gold gleaming half-moon seemed to be winking at all of us scurrying up and down Madison Avenue. The temperature has risen above freezing for the first time this week. I think of him,

*doubtlessly out somewhere, perhaps walking too, the moon track-
ing him just as it is tracking me. I think about the meridian we
two mature people had crossed at 10:30 on that night. Had we
had our affair with wisdom? With awkwardness? Maturity? Im-
maturity? Good sense? Bad judgment? Love? Lack of love? Kindness? Unkindness? Courage? Cowardice? I need time to unknot
the various threads.*

*(This is for you, Alison, for your inquiry. I hope it helps.)
Since everything has a beginning, middle and an end, for better or
worse, the delicate, hand-blown glass of my affair did too. The
bridge of my transition since Misha's death was crossed. Ed had
been the handrail I held as I crossed the wobbling expanse from
dead love to new love, no sex to sex. Ed was dear and sexy
though, quite honestly, the inner ballet of his heart remains a
mystery to me. He was easy to love. I hope he'll be easy to
unlove.*

*FYI: I have a sense that, in middle age, after a battery of affairs
on his side and the earth-shattering death of dear Misha on mine,
Ed and I had courageously coauthored a work of mood, psychology, sound, light, shadow, color, sense, nuance. Even though it's
over, we share, will always share, its copyright, its royalties, the
richness of its beginning, its middle and its nocturnal end.*

Paula phones when she's back in the city and, wrapped up in
scarfs, gloves and hats because the wind is raw, we take a walk
along the Hudson River at the Chelsea Pier, around the comic, six-
story driving range. Then we return to my apartment for coffee.
She takes a plastic container from her carryall. With it, a book, *She
Comes First: The Thinking Man's Guide to Pleasuring a Woman* by
Ian Kerner.

"It's a manifesto on cunnilingus. I kid you not. The writer's a sex therapist. He thinks that Viagra is the most awful thing that could have happened to women because it refocuses sex back to the penis, away from oral sex. He thinks men need to know how to pleasure women orally, and this book provides instructions. Literally!"

We look at each other, eyebrows raised. She puts the container on my table. "To have with our coffee. They're gluten-free muffins." She removes the lid. "I baked them."

After I've brewed coffee, she offers me a muffin. It has a flavor that's piquant but also spicy; the texture—crunchy, chewy.

"They're unusual. What's in them?"

"Cinnamon. Apple. Zucchini. Walnuts. Orange zest. Plenty of it. What makes them unusual is that I've added coconut flakes."

We chew and sip. She tells me about a new violin she's buying with money from her dead husband's insurance. I return the envelope containing the notebook and tell her that she'd moved me and that I'm sorry.

"Don't be," she says. "Things went as far as they could go for Ed and I."

"Are you bruised by what happened?"

"Yes and no. The pain and sadness the ending gave me has been mostly mollified since I wrote the words you read. It was as if I began a new gastronomic adventure with Ed. It whetted my taste for love and sex and romance. He primed my pump. After Misha died, I didn't know if I could go through it all again. But having such good sex with Ed made me realize that sex is a Pandora's box, in a good sense."

She nibbles on a muffin.

"For better or worse, the lid is open and God knows what will jump out at me next. If I'm lucky, maybe I'll do better in the compatibility area . . . the oral sex area."

She giggles.

"Maybe I'll learn to make things even better from books like this and—like the orange zest in these muffins—I intend to grate as much zest as possible into that part of my life."

She puts the lid on the container and slides it into her carryall.

180-Degree Turns

I've taken Amtrak's Lake Shore Limited. Tomorrow morning, in Chicago, I'll walk over to the Art Institute, have a look, have lunch, then catch the Southwest Chief for Los Angeles. I'm counting on spending three solitary nights and days on the train, reading and staring out at the changing landscape. In the first hours of traveling up along the Hudson River, I sit in the overheated café car reading Paul Theroux's *Dark Star Safari* and pour cranberry juice (it's all they have) over plastic cupfuls of ice. Between reading and sipping, I gaze in blank reverie out the window at the wintry beauty of the Hudson River. At one point I carry a tray for an eighty-something woman with narrow shoulders and silvery hair cut in a pageboy that makes her look very much like a geriatric June Allyson. (Or, for those who don't remember June Allyson, a geriatric Drew Barrymore.) On her tray is a Sanka and a cinnamon roll that she's quartered. There's a pillow tucked under her arm.

There are some people who have no sense that someone reading a book might be busy. She's one of these people. She offers me a quarter of the sweet roll with a dry voice, plops down her pillow, and sits across from me on top of it. I'd been saving this book for just such a train ride, had just marked—*aging can be startling too; the sapling grown into a great oak, the vast edifice made into a ruin*—but I give in to the cinnamon roll.

"Where are you going?" she inquires.

"California."

"My. That's quite a trip. What do you do?"

"I write books."

Her Windex-blue eyes narrow.

"What are you writing about?"

"Suffice to say I'm writing about the heart."

"Perhaps you know about this. They've discovered a new, uh, device. It's for the human heart that's enlarged or maybe sagging. It's like a pair of support hose."

"Support hose?"

"You know, panty hose. Support hose for the heart. It wraps around the heart and holds it together, supports it."

"I'm not writing about medical issues related to the human heart."

"Then what? You look like a doctor."

"I do? I'm writing about middle-aged people and love."

"How sad."

She now has my full attention.

"Sad?"

She doesn't answer directly. Instead, she explains that she'd been visiting her daughter Gwendolyn in Albany. It seems that Gwendolyn divorced her first husband when she was middle-aged but has remarried.

"Great."

"Is it?"

"What's wrong with the new husband?"

In a flat voice she says, "He's a Democrat!"

At this point I close my book entirely and ask, "Beside being a Democrat, what's wrong with the new husband?"

I hope I've kept any tone of irony out of my voice.

"Don't let me get started. She's turned things inside out. She used to be so normal—a Republican like her father and me, sang in the church choir. Until she met him. She calls him Snoopy. They believe they were personages in the Old Testament in a past life. A psychic told them that they originally met in Babylon long before Christ. But if that isn't enough, they collect teddy bears and stuffed animals."

I'm rapt.

"I counted seventy-five stuffed animals. If that isn't bad enough they dress them up and talk to them. They brought one to the dinner table and sat it on a chair. I moved it—it was a gray wolf—so I could sit down, and my son-in-law said in a little voice that pretended to be a wolf's voice, 'Hey, Grandma, be gentle with me,' and my daughter chimed in, in a little-girl voice, 'Sorry, Ecclesiastes!' Then in a normal voice she said, 'Mother, that's Ecclesiastes' chair.' Then Snoopy went into the kitchen and brought a kitchen chair out into the dining room for *me*, and the wolf remained in the good dining room chair that should have been mine for the entire meal."

I ask, "Do you think she's happy having a new life that's so different from her earlier life?"

"If bringing handfuls of autumn leaves into the living room and throwing them all around, and playing jacks and tops on the floor with a man who has arthritis is happiness, then I guess they are. Her effort to explain was to say, 'Mother, Jesus said we can't get into the Kingdom of Heaven until we are like children.'"

I empty my plastic cup of juice, ask if she'd like another cup of Sanka.

"One's my limit. But this train doesn't go to California!"

"In Chicago I change trains."

"I get off in Chicago."

It has gotten absolutely black outside; the café car is closing for an hour to give the barman a break. I hear the train whistling urgently as it speeds past clanging barriers while red lights flash. I offer to walk her to her compartment. She holds on to my sleeve. She jokes that, like the song says, we'll be having our ham and eggs in Carolina but she substitutes Chicago for Carolina.

"Like Lazarus risen from the ashes"

Dan Fante is a fourth-generation Californian living close to the Pacific Ocean, in Southern California. His new wife Ayrin will shortly give birth to a baby. Dan is the son of John Fante, the *noir* writer first published in 1932 in the *American Mercury* who is sometimes called the Italian Hemingway. Born in Colorado in 1909, an alcoholic who had a tempestuous relationship with his own father, John Fante had a career that was a roller coaster, which went from fame to obscurity and back to fame. When John was in his late forties, he was diagnosed with diabetes that caused him to go blind when he was sixty-nine. Because his wife, the poet Joyce Fante, was willing to help him, he was able to write one final novel, called *Dreams from Bunker Hill*.

Dan, the second of Joyce and John's four children, had a wish to follow in his father's footsteps and become a writer even as a boy. Due to alcohol his ambition was thwarted. Finally, at age forty-six, his lifelong ambition was realized when his first novel, *Chump Change*, was completed. His second novel, *Mooch*, followed three years later and has been optioned by Danny De Vito for a film adaptation. The third novel in the trilogy is called *Spitting Off Tall Buildings*. It was published in 2000. Dan has also published a book of poems, and soon a book of short stories titled *Corksucker* will be published by Sun Dog Press. His books have been translated into twelve languages.

We set up our appointment by telephone. It's a few weeks before the birth of his baby, and since it's been a while since I've seen him face-to-face, I ask on the telephone, "Do you still have the earring in your ear?"

"No. I wear a red stone in my nose. I had a nose ring first, but since my new life began I've had a diamond stud in my nose. That's what you remember but it wasn't in my ear it was in my nose. . . ."

Of course. It was his nose.

"To celebrate my marriage, my wonderful life, the diamond stud was traded in for a red stone."

Dan's "wonderful life" has been like Lazarus, risen from the ashes of a vastly different, mostly unwonderful, earlier life. Our face-to-face interview is convivial and light. Dan's an easy guy to talk to. The first thing he tells me is that his history with women has been poor indeed.

"Why?"

"Simply put, because of my alcohol problem, I really never allowed myself to sustain anything that would improve my self-esteem. I was good at a number of different things but I would drink and screw them up. Being the son of a hypercritical guy, I was also the recipient of some of his angst. I moved to New York at nineteen where I began the struggle to get an identity of my own. Almost immediately I married and a child was born. A son. The marriage lasted about five years."

At the time, Dan was driving a cab. He had ambition but no direction. He drove a cab for seven years in Manhattan, the Bronx and Brooklyn. In those years the fares were very low but the tips for short trips were very good.

"So I worked Madison Avenue. Usually if I took an eighty-cent fare, I'd get a buck and a half tip. I moved from the Bronx to a hotel called The Pickwick Arms on Fifty-first between Second and Third. I'd get off work at five-thirty. There was a Blarney Stone at Fifty-sixth and Broadway. I was trying to write but my drinking was quite out of control. I was out of control sexually. Needless to say, my wife, my son and I no longer lived together."

He gathers his thoughts.

"Around 1971, I couldn't drive a cab anymore, I got to a place where I hated it, I could no longer do the hours. There was no air-conditioning in those days. It was a brutal kind of job. I went to work as a chauffeur. I worked eighty hours a week as a chauffeur. I had a blue polyester suit void of any natural fiber. You could stand it up in the corner. I had a clip-on tie, a Greek seaman's cap. All very nice. At this point, I lived in this little apartment on Sixty-fourth and Second above a hamburger place. The apartment had never had a phone. When I wasn't driving my limo I was drinking."

It's not hard to imagine Dan's seedy side, though these days he's scrubbed and pink and wears a Hawaiian shirt open at the collar.

"I was in a relationship with a woman who was on cocaine and black beauties and we were at each other's throats constantly. There were no children, thank God. Then I went into partnership with the owner of the limo company. I moved to the West Coast to open the L.A. arm of the company. Within a year it was the most successful limo company in L.A. Suddenly I was showered with money and success. We had the entire rock 'n' roll clientele of Columbia Records. We drove all the rock groups. We drove Rod Stewart, Eric Clapton, everyone wanted us."

He had the first stretch limousines in L.A. with pastel colors. One limo had eight pounds of crushed pearl in the paint.

"We called the car Pearl. It was magnificent."

But his drinking and drug use escalated.

"I had sex with anyone and everyone. I told my business partner, 'Buy me out.' He came at me with a handful of money, which was about twenty percent of what the company was worth, but I took it. After that, I rented a house in Laurel Canyon on a street called Wonderland Avenue which is, in effect, the country even though it's five minutes from Hollywood. It's up in the hills. Quickly I got into a terrible financial situation. My car was repossessed. I was getting in a lot of trouble, getting DWIs, driving drunk, hitting parked cars. I wound up homeless sleeping on a friend's couch. I had to find work and tried selling a door-to-door dating service in Hawthorne and Torrance. It was so fucking hot. I'm wearing a suit and tie and going into people's homes. People were throwing me out. Then I went to work for someone who hired indigents in a converted motel on Motor Avenue with five other down-and-outs selling office supplies by phone."

"Oh. I think someone like you called me once and it cost me five hundred dollars."

"This work is called telemarketing. I had another wife at this point. That was the early eighties. That marriage lasted about ten months. As soon as I started on the phone, I was unstoppable. I had the gift to slam people on the phone. Quickly I had a house in Venice, a brand-new Porsche, an aerobics teacher girlfriend . . . another disastrous relationship. But—though I didn't know it at the time—I was bottoming out. It wasn't until I stopped drinking at forty-two that I was able to stabilize emotionally."

He'd been in therapy for fourteen or fifteen years, had been in the thicket of despair and had three suicide attempts that he can remember.

"I had sex with everything except a 1950 Ford. The monumental thing that occurred in my life, stopping drinking, didn't happen un-til I was—if you will—into my second act. When I stopped drinking at last I stopped the major part of my self-destruction. I thought I was just a psycho. No shrink ever said, 'You're an alcoholic.' Not once. Once I was sober through the help of a twelve-step group, an emo-tional leveling was possible. . . . My relationship with women . . . with everybody . . . with God . . . began to change."

There's emotion in his voice, softness in his face.

"Having a spiritual aspect in my life changed everything. The great gift is that I've finally found a marriage—this is my fourth, by the way—that fulfills every need. And, I've found what I intended to do—what God intended for me to do—with my life."

"Would you say your novels are biographical?"

"Oh yeah—autobiographical—similar to the kind of stuff my dad wrote but more honest, gut level. In 1935 you couldn't be as graphic as you can today. My stuff is similar to Hubert Selby, Jr., to Bukowski, although I'm a better writer than Bukowski."

"A lot funnier."

"You're not going to find too many yuks and chuckles in Bukowski."

"I laughed a lot when reading your novels. I saw your play, *The Closer*, about telemarketing. I laughed like hell watching it."

"The *L.A. Times* put it at the top of their list of plays for the year. It ran for two and a half years. I've written a play for my wife that—I hope—she'll be doing down the road. There's an ease and comfort to this relationship. I no longer even want to get angry, have adrenaline rushes."

"Is it possible that you've got a closeness in this marriage that your parents had in theirs late in life? I take it your mother and father were very close at the end of your father's life."

"Your reference to my parent's relationship is correct. While my father was blind and a double amputee, my mom, at the cost of her own health, cared for him. For months he would wake at night in a blind delirium and not know where he was. Mom was always asleep down the hall only a few feet away. When he regained himself after months of semi-confusion, he was able to dictate his last book to her word for word. Remarkably, his prose was flawless. Not one word was changed. He *saw* the entire manuscript before he *said* it out loud. I was there and witnessed many of those dictation sessions."

"Amazing."

"I was just talking about my distaste for adrenaline rushes to a friend who I exercise with. We walk every day down at the beach a couple of miles, forty-five minutes."

"Are you planning on being in the delivery room with your wife?"

"I hope so."

"That's the plan?"

"Oh, my gosh."

"First time?"

"It's so much different. I'm just so grateful and thrilled at my age—I'm sixty—to have my health. I just lost another one of my friends . . ."

"They're really tumbling. Mine too. One of mine just committed suicide."

"Normal people in their forties and fifties are witnessing their parents' getting old plus a smattering of deaths. But people in twelve-step programs—people who've lived hard—they've seen a lot of death . . . people normally in the prime of life. I am really guarded and jealous and grateful about my health. I'm actually in very good health for my age. My liver is healed. No damage. I take stuff for cholesterol. Lipitor. My blood pressure's fine. I exercise. I had a real identity crisis. I didn't know what I was sexually but when I got sober that changed. My sexual identity is completely heterosexual now. It's all wonderful. In truth I was never homosexual, I was omnisexual."

"Is your wife happy?"

"Oh, yeah. This is her first marriage. My wife lived in New York, Paris, London. My wife and I come from very different backgrounds—she's a runway model, a print model, an actress. Our connection is the theater. We've got a strong connection there. I'm a fourth-generation Californian."

"Were you married in the church?"

"No. We were married in Vegas. The baby's due in a couple of weeks. I write at home in the morning. My wife is now in the last two weeks of her job. It's all good."

· · ·

And, right on target a few weeks later, he e-mails to say that his wife, Ayrin, has given birth. I immediately send him an e-mail by way of congratulations and get his reply:

> Thanks, Alison . . .
> My arms hold breath
> Life and death
> And the song is everywhere
> Perfection is everywhere
> I will never be the same again
> Never again
> df

Ayrin, Michelangelo, Joyce and Dan

"It's a boy. We've called him Michelangelo. I'm his during-the-day caregiver. The enclosed photo is of me, my wife, Ayrin, Michelangelo and my mother, Joyce Fante. My mother's 91 and still correcting my grammar."

"I never felt that way before"

A ceremony is being prepared; has been designed around the sun that will set at 6:14. The plan is that the sun will sink into the horizon at a certain moment at the end of the ceremony. The house is just outside of Santa Fe and a white tent has been set up so that the guests will face the sunset; the couple will face the guests. Judy Nix, who's dark, with brown eyes, will wear a black and gold and red chenille jacket with black hostess pants. Her blond partner will wear a blue jacket, also a kind of chenille.

During our interview, Judy describes her partner's eyes: "If Mary Ellen is wearing green, then her eyes are green; if she has on blue, then they're blue."

That day, the day of their commitment ceremony, they are blue.

Mary Ellen Degnan was raised a Catholic in Newton, Massachusetts, the only daughter of Irish immigrants who already had three sons when she was born. The man she married in 1965 was thirty-one, eight and a half years older than her. He was a very conservative businessman raised in Grosse Pointe, Michigan, who flew his own airplane. The couple settled in Dallas, Texas, where, as Mary Ellen explains, "If you want to be an entrepreneur, you can do it easier in Texas than in Boston."

Within five and a half years the couple had four children. They acquired a second home, a lake house, flew their own airplane, and sent their children to private schools. When the children needed her less, Mary Ellen became involved with nonprofit groups; quite soon, she was asked by one of them to get off the board and become executive director. The marriage lasted twenty-five years and six days, ending in an acrimonious divorce.

Judy describes her Dallas childhood as "an idyllic Cinderella kind of childhood, pretty sheltered, pretty protected." An only child from an Episcopalian family with Lebanese roots, she came out as a debutante, then went to Mills College in Oakland, California. At first she worked as a secretary to a stockbroker but advanced quickly to a job in a brokerage firm. Soon she got her broker's license and, by the early seventies, was offered a post as a securities trader with the third-largest bank in Dallas.

"How did you feel being a woman in a man's field?" I ask.

"I took to it like a duck to water. I loved it."

Judy continued working until, at twenty-seven, she married another Texan. The man she married was "doing very well in business. The first two years just rocked along. No big ups or downs. We had our son after four years in 1974. The marriage changed after our son was born. The marriage lasted twenty years and nine months."

Judy says about her youth, "I hadn't dated a lot, I was pretty naive."

Mary Ellen describes herself as "outgoing, liking people."

In her high school yearbook, Mary Ellen was named Most Popular. Neither of them recalls having the slightest hint of, or attraction to, a person of the same sex. At fifty, that changed.

Mary Ellen: "At the time of my divorce, I had no notion of my own self. When it got out that I was getting a divorce, I began dating a lot. This experience reconfirmed that I was—am—a desirable woman. It was crazy and fun. At no time did I ever feel anything other than being totally interested in men. I'd known Judy for fifteen years but not well. We'd done a lot of civic and cultural work together in Dallas. I admired her because she'd really made a name for herself. She divorced just after I did. We had lunch occasionally."

Judy: "Getting divorced was the most liberating decision I'd ever made. I'd been in therapy for many years and realized I'd lived the first forty years of my life in neutral. I wasn't going forward, I wasn't going back. I was idling and letting time go by. I also learned that I'd put all my emotions in neutral too. I could function . . . sure . . . I never missed a beat but insofar as truly engaging emotionally with anyone—not just a partner but anyone, my son, friends, people—I know now that I didn't fully engage. I was reserved. I held back. People thought I was aloof or shy. I knew that that was not where I wanted to be emotionally in my life. This is what finally gave me the courage and initiative to change the marriage situation. I felt it was holding me back."

After her divorce, Judy dated a fellow she'd known about a year. It was a wonderful post-divorce relationship.

"It sort of gave me the feeling of being an attractive woman again, which I hadn't had in a long time. I'd known Mary Ellen since the early eighties, we saw each other at civic things, always enjoyed each other's company. One of my friends had said to me, 'You should get together with Mary Ellen because she's really enjoying being divorced.'"

Her speech has a Texas twang to it.

"We reconnected in '92 ran into each other at an exhibition called 'Catherine the Great.' I said, 'Maybe we can go out and have lunch sometime and you can help me get used to this situation?' That's when the friendship really began. For the next year or so we lunched, compared war stories about our ex-husbands, about our post-divorce affairs. Our friendship became better and better, closer and closer. When I decided that I was going to plan my fiftieth birthday in Santa Fe, Mary Ellen was the first one I called. I thought, This is odd because I didn't know her that well. But that's all I thought about it."

Mary Ellen: "One day Judy called me at my office and said, 'I'm having my fiftieth birthday party and I'm having it in Santa Fe. I'd like to invite you.' 'When is it?' I asked. 'Late September.' 'You're pretty organized,' I said, since this was April. She told me later that I was the first person she'd called because she definitely wanted me to be there. We're always saying, 'Who started this?'"

"Ha."

"It is funny. The weekend in Sante Fe was wonderful. There were eight friends. The first unusual thing was when some of us went walking to see the trees turning, I looked around for Judy, couldn't spot her. Then, I saw her walking toward us. When she got close, I could tell she was getting emotional. I said, 'Are you thinking about what I'm thinking about?' She said, 'Yes.' I said, 'Is it that you're overwhelmed by this?' She said, 'Yes, I am. I can't say how lucky I feel that all these great people have come all the way from Dallas to celebrate my birthday with me.'"

There's ebullience in her voice.

"I did this spontaneous thing. It's hilarious. Judy has a beautiful head of hair . . . that's one of the things that was very attractive. She has great big brown eyes. She was wearing a brown leather headband to keep her hair out of her eyes. She sat down at the side of the slope and I leaned over and kissed her on the top of her headband. I said, 'You're just a fabulous person. That's why we're all here.' There was absolutely nothing intended in that gesture. That moment passed, and we drove back down the mountain and I felt this energy. She told me later, she did too."

That night, after their last dinner together in town, and be-cause Mary Ellen had previously broken her foot and it was still healing, Judy drove Mary Ellen back. They sat outside the B&B. Everyone was waiting inside to tell Judy what a great weekend they'd had, and to go up to bed.

Mary Ellen: "We sat out in the car in the parking lot and talked for about an hour and a half. No one knew where we were. We just talked and talked. But what we were realizing was that we didn't want it to end. Both of us tell each other that it was clear at that moment."

Judy: "I'd cried with joy at having my pals with me in Sante Fe but there was this other special energy with Mary Ellen that I didn't feel with the others. I thought, This is strange! and yet it wasn't strange. It was strange in that I'd never felt it before, but it wasn't strange because she's a very open and loving and giving per-son and I was very attracted to that."

To Mary Ellen: "How old were you at the time?"

"Fifty-one and a half, there's eighteen months between Judy and I. I hadn't ever felt like that. It was a physical sensation. I hadn't felt that way probably about anyone ever. Sex is one thing, but to have a real, true, strong energy is another. I could feel the energy going back and forth between us. I knew she could too but neither of us said anything because we were both scared to death."

She pauses for breath.

"The next morning, she was sitting at the breakfast table in the B&B when I came down. The minute I saw those eyes we both knew. We just knew. It was frightening for both of us. Judy was scheduled to come to my lake house the following weekend, but now everything had changed between us."

Judy: "I realized that there was something more than a fun weekend between us. That was the beginning of taking our relationship to a different level. It was extraordinarily frightening to me in the beginning because it felt so good, totally different than anything I'd ever felt before."

The next weekend, they drove down to the lake house on a Saturday evening. On the way they started talking around what they'd both felt so strongly.

Judy: "By the time we got to the lake house we were talking about it openly like, 'What is this? What's going on?' We talked about it very late into the night then she went into her guest room and I went into mine."

Mary Ellen: "Both of us lay there wide-eyed all night . . . wondering. The next day we talked about it again ad nauseam. Later in the afternoon I said, 'Well, I'm going in to take a nap. And, if you want to join me, you can.' The rest is our personal story."

"Had you had any drinks? Anything?"

"Nothing. No. It was the middle of the day. The energy was overwhelming, that's all I can say. It still is. It's been eleven years almost. Our lives changed that day."

Judy: "At this point in time, because I'd made good progress in my therapy group, a graduation date had been set for me. When things began to happen with Mary Ellen, I went into the group and talked about it and suddenly graduation was off. It dawned on me that I'd been repressing a lot of things for a long time. So at this point . . . after the Santa Fe weekend, although I'd made good progress in my therapy, I knew I wasn't ready yet to stop. The next step of a sexual relationship with Mary Ellen started, so I talked about this phenomenon with the group. All of a sudden a lot of things that had happened to my marriage and divorce—about where I was and who I was—made more sense. The first year and a half of our relationship was very traumatic. We were up and down, in and out, on and off. I said over and over, 'I can't do this. I just can't.'"

Mary Ellen: "Twice during that time, we broke up. At one point, for six months. The arrangement was that we were going to 'be normal,' and we were going to date men. We did that. We tried to be friends by telephone but that didn't work out very well. It was an awkward time. In the meantime, I became involved with a widower. He was wealthy, attractive, wanted to go around the world with me. Judy called me up, was outraged. I said, 'Remember the agreement we had?' When I broke up with him, I called her. She said, 'Thanks for calling but I'm getting on with my life.' She was so angry with me."

Judy: "It took me a very long time to get past all the baggage that I had carried with me given my traditional family, the conservative Lebanese family background. My father had passed away in 1972. He wasn't in the picture. My mother lived almost until she was ninety. She was a constant worry to me. She guessed it and I didn't deny it, and she threw all kinds of fits and threatened to cut me out of her will. I said, 'Do what you want but I'd hate you to penalize your grandson, my son, at my expense, so why don't you leave it to him directly.' She hung up on me but in the end she did not follow through. It was pretty traumatic for both of us actually, but the fact is that the attraction was huge and it was way beyond anything I'd ever felt before . . . way beyond."

The one thing Judy had learned in therapy was to pay attention to her feelings instead of putting the emotions on hold. So the struggle continued.

"Finally—gradually—I got beyond my upbringing, my parents'

feelings. Then, after two more years of therapy, I did actually graduate and Mary Ellen came to the graduation. It was wonderful. I
had a lot of help. I have to give a lot of credit to my therapist, to
my group. Mary Ellen and I were together a couple of years before
we decided to move here to Santa Fe. About five years ago we
bought the house but continued to commute and work in Dallas.
By then we were living fairly openly."

Mary Ellen: "We got to a point where we weren't going to worry
if anyone was going to hire us in Dallas. I'm happy to tell you that
just last year a very well-known arts group hired the both of us.
So Dallas is loosening up. We found out who our friends are. I told
my children, my son first. He'd already figured it out. He's the
youngest. He said, 'You're a wonderful lady and she's a wonderful
lady and who cares.' My daughters had already figured it out. When
I told them, they said, 'Mom, this is the nineties. That's great. We
like her.' "

A ll five of their adult children have come to the commitment
ceremony. Rabbi Malka Drucker will officiate at the service.
Rabbi Drucker calls herself a trans-denominational rabbi. She was
ordained in 1998 at the Academy for Jewish Religion based in New
York. Since her ordination Rabbi Drucker has lived in Santa Fe
working as a rabbi. (She also happens to be a much-published
writer of books for adults and children; her latest book is *White
Fire: A Portrait of Women Spiritual Leaders in America*.)

Judy and Mary Ellen wanted a spiritual leader of sorts to officiate and Malka, who had presided at several other lesbian cere-
monies, agreed to do it. Rabbi Drucker told them she would design

a ceremony that wasn't in any particular faith using bits from Christian tradition, from Jewish tradition, and perhaps from other traditions, including some of her own design.

When the ceremony begins, the five adult children accompany their mothers down the aisle and encircle them as the self-styled vows are spoken. Each woman has written her own lines. The ceremony in part:

Judy: "Bind me as a seal upon your heart, a sign upon your arm. Sear my emblem deep into your skin."

Mary Ellen: "For love is strong as death, harsh as the grave. Its tongues are flames, a fierce and holy blaze."

Together: "Together, in suffering and joy, I will share with you my body, my feelings, my thought, my spirit."

Toward the end of the ceremony, the rabbi turns to the guests and says, "We all love weddings because we witness the miracle of two finding each other and especially these two who waited so long. Their wedding tells us to keep hope, have courage, and above all, take the risk that comes with love."

The sun has begun to set.

The rabbi continues: "I invite you to remember your own love, your own dream of love, and take the power of your vision and let it become a blessing for Mary Ellen and Judy, who will join us with the most appropriate music for their procession, 'Ode to Joy.'"

Judy chokes up when she tells me about that day.

"There was not a dry eye in the crowd at the end of the thing. It was wonderful, just wonderful. Then—like newlyweds everywhere—we went off on a honeymoon to Europe."

"We were shocked how much we loved it"

F or many years, if you asked my family what was their saddest day they'd say, 'The day Cheryl left home for the convent to become Sister Cheryl Donahue.'"

"Do you mean that you weren't able to see your family?"

Sister Cheryl Donahue

"It's kind of funny because as time went on and the rules got lax, I was able to see my family more regularly. I loved the different places I lived while I was with the sisters."

Cheryl lived in upstate New York for three years; then, in Georgia, she was the director of religious education and adult education. At that point, she had gone back to school and gotten a master's degree in adult education; she taught elementary school for a while, doing vocational work with young women who showed an interest in wanting to become sisters.

"Was it a strict order?"

"It's certainly not cloistered. After Vatican Two they started to lighten up a bit, the church became more a part of the world around, not just tied up with itself."

Cheryl Kane joined the order of the Missionary Franciscan Sisters of the Immaculate Conception when she was nineteen. She stayed with them for twenty-three years. While she was a nun she began to work in a homeless shelter run by the Boston Health Care for the Homeless Program. She went to nursing school to get a degree in nursing when she was forty-three. Today, more than ten years later, she's part of an outreach team for that same organization. Night and day, winter and summer, you can find Cheryl, either alone or with one or more members of her team, somewhere out on the streets of Boston.

"I have the best job in the whole world. It's something that totally feeds my soul. I work with homeless men and women who—for whatever reason—won't come into the shelter. So I visit them on the street. I work in a multidisciplinary team. It's made up of a doctor, a physician's assistant, a psychologist, and a social worker. There are other outreach teams from some of the neighboring agencies. They aren't medical, so if they run across someone with a medical problem, they'll page me or someone on our team, and we'll go out onto the street to find and try to assess the person."

I ask for a description of some of what she does.

"Sometimes I might take out sutures. Today I cleaned a wound, dressed it. It might mean taking someone to detox. It might mean 9ll'ing someone to the hospital. I never know. Someone might be having some psychological issue. During the day we go on foot all over Boston. At night there's a van that combs the city. They provide blankets and sandwiches, and someone from our medical team usually rides on the van as well. Sometimes it's me."

"Does this mean that you get to know a lot of the same people for years?"

"Oh, absolutely. We really do. It's critical critical critical that we establish a relationship with these people. Our patients are so much on the fringe of society and have really broken a lot of their human bridges. They're very nontrusting and many of them have mental illness as well. Until we can establish a bond of trust, it's really not until that happens, that we can begin to do our work.

When somebody trusts us enough to tell us their stories and struggles, then they'll usually tell us some of their medical needs. Their
lives are so chaotic that very often taking care of medical concerns
is the last thing on the list. It's like, 'Where am I going to sleep
tonight? Where am I going to eat today?'"

"Is there a way for someone in a crisis to search you out?"

"It's kind of funny. The community on the street is very, very
strong. Lots of times when I'm out walking someone will say to me,
'Oh, so-and-so's been sick all night. You'd better go and find him.'
At which point I will. Last week I got a page from one of our patients saying she was really, really sick. She didn't know what to do,
and could I meet her at one of the parks."

"Do you have much of a success rate getting people off the
streets or is that not really a goal? Or, do you just try to keep people
as well as you can?"

"If somebody completes a whole regime of antibiotics, that's a
huge success. There's a guy we've been trying for weeks to get to go
to the shelter. Today he agreed. We were so excited about that. We
also have a twenty-four-hour medical-care respite program—the
Barbara McInnis House—for homeless men and women who are
too sick for the shelter, but not sick enough for the hospital."

"What sorts of illnesses?"

"It could be somebody dually diagnosed with diabetes or cardiac
issues, someone having asthma that's out of line, a woman with a
high-risk pregnancy, someone with a broken limb; during winter
people who have frostbite or the flu. Recently, we've been ponder-
ing end-of-life care for our homeless patients who have no family
or support. Here in Boston if you're staying in a shelter you have to
be out by seven A.M. If you have any of the things I just mentioned,
it's hard to be hanging out on the street all day."

"Let's turn to when you decided to end your life as a nun. Was that the happiest day for your family, the day you came out?"

She pauses, then replies, "It was a hard decision. I loved the sisters. I loved the work but by my early forties I wanted to work with the homeless in a fuller way, meaning that I wouldn't have to be tied down to the structure that the sisters expected, like being home on time, which was an important part of our lives."

"Did it take a long time to decide?"

"Yeah. It took a very long time. I needed help to realize that I wasn't breaking my relationship and commitment to God, that I was just changing the way I was going to live it out. Once I got that out of my head and into my heart, it was okay."

"So it was gradual?"

"Very gradual."

All the while she was mulling over her decision, she had been speaking to someone who was supposed to help with the process, who was more objective.

"While I was doing this vocation work, I had several other counterparts who did the same work. One of the people I worked with was a Jesuit priest."

"His name?"

"Jim. Father Jim Kane. We became really good friends."

Jim Kane was working with candidates who wanted to join religious orders. When it came time for Cheryl to make her decision, she talked to Jim quite a lot.

"Making this decision was a huge struggle. He was very helpful. He helped me process my thoughts. Unbeknownst to me, this was a struggle that he too had been having for many, many years, on whether or not to leave the Jesuits. He didn't tell me at the time. The year I left the Franciscans was also the year Jim left the Jesuits.

The next year his mother was sick, he went down to Connecticut to care for her. After she died, he came back to Boston."

I've been speaking to Cheryl on the telephone. At this point in our talk, I've warmed to her.

"When Jim left the Jesuits, I was just starting nursing school at Boston College. When he came back to town, he started working at Boston College and we began to have dinner together . . . as lay people. We used to joke with each other saying, 'Oh, my God, if you hear me tell you I'm getting married, shoot me.' Neither of us wanted to be tied down. We became really, really good friends. Nothing romantic. We saw each other all the time. We'd have dinner together. Then we started realizing what a real comfort it was . . . to talk . . . to be together. Our backgrounds were so similar even though he was older than I was by seven years. And then we married."

"Did that surprise your family?"

"Yeah. The year before we got married, they could see how happy we were, how much we enjoyed each other."

Cheryl and Jim—Act II

"Tell me about your married life."

"We both just loved being married. We were shocked how much we loved it. We were crazy about each other. We'd been married about one and a half years when one day I picked up the telephone, and it was Jim saying he had a terrible headache. As he spoke he began repeating himself, seemed to be forgetting names of people he knew intimately. I could tell that something was very wrong. I asked if he knew my name. He said, 'No. But I know you're my wife.'"

My heart clenches; I hadn't expected her story to take such a turn.

"Before I could get to him, he had a massive seizure. An ambulance took him to a hospital. Very quickly he was diagnosed with a deadly brain tumor. I was in my last year of nursing school when he was diagnosed. Jim had been a very, very healthy man throughout his life; it was almost impossible to believe."

"Were you angry?"

"We had both found what we wanted to do . . . found each other. Of course I accused God. Of course I was angry. We'd had so little time together, he was a young man in his early fifties. How could this have happened? Though his type of tumor is deadly, the doctors decided to do brain surgery. To our amazement, after a lengthy post-op convalescence, very gradually, Jim began to get well. It seemed like a miracle. He was a runner who'd run ten marathons and had put his running shoes back on. He began to train for the marathon that would take place in spring. Of course I thanked God."

Things began to seem normal all summer, all fall. Winter came. It seemed like it would be a joyful Christmas, but when Jim went for a routine MRI, the news was bleak.

"Not only had the tumor reappeared but it was rapidly growing, was inoperable. We both knew what that meant. Again my faith in God crumbled."

Once Jim was terminal, Cheryl took a leave from her job so she could be with him night and day—as nurse, as wife—for whatever time he had left.

"Very quickly I knew that I couldn't be angry at God and ask him for strength at the same time. I realized how much I needed God . . . much more than God needed me. Suffice to say, I'd had a lifetime of trust in God. My faith hadn't deserted me. I knew Jim's hadn't either when he began having visions of angels. He saw them as very beautiful, as very loving. They were in the room with us near the end."

Her voice thickens.

"Those last months together were the most intimate of our marriage. I think of it as sacred. Of course he wouldn't be running in the Boston Marathon, but many of his friends did and, still wearing running clothes, came to visit Jim after the race, told him all about the race. They brought the excitement of the marathon into the room, surrounded Jim with it. A few hours later he died. It was as if he'd laced on his running shoes and run off toward God . . . had his own race to finish."

Again there's silence, then she changes the subject, speaks about a woman she's run into today who'd lived on the streets for fifteen years. The woman was on her way to speak at a conference on the homeless in Washington, D.C.

"I don't know what it is . . . what gives you the inner strength to be able to follow through with something you need to do. Whatever it was for her, that's the thing I can relate to. Something happens inside that moves you in a direction."

"Fate?"

She doesn't respond to my question, instead returns to the subject of Jim's death.

"After Jim died, the only thing that kept me going was my work with the homeless. If I hadn't had my work, I don't know how I would have gotten through those first months, first years. He died in April of 1998. It was my need to be of help to people who needed help that had attracted me to the work of the Franciscan Sisters early on, it was that same need to help people that ended up helping me to survive. It wasn't until I was over forty that I knew what it was to fall in love with a man. It happened."

A few months later I speak on the phone with Cheryl Kane again to catch up on her news. She tells me:

"I'm selling my big house in Milton and moving to Dorchester to the old Baker Chocolate Factory. Recently I began going to a Friday evening dance near where I live. I like to dance. Jim's been dead for over seven years now. You know how crazy I was about him. Just crazy. But . . . I've been dancing with a man who goes there, we enjoy each other's company. We've begun to date. Mind you, he's one hundred percent different than Jim. But he's a terrific man. His name is Russell. He's a barber and we like dancing together."

ACT TWO, SCENE FOUR

Comfort and Stability

I sort through notes in the file folder because it's bitter cold outside. I read that, in the view of Martha Horton, therapist and author of *Growing Up in Adulthood*, maturity ensures us "a confidence in all the emotions we have, fearing none." Further, maturity promises "a life of wholeness . . . if one's willing to go for it. That's all our emotions, including tenderness, desire, passion, Eros." It strikes me that in our youth-centered culture, the word "maturity" is not necessarily cultivated as a desirable quality. I peruse another source—Plato's *The Symposium*. It characterizes love as "the most ancient of the gods, the most honored, and the most effective in enabling human beings to acquire courage and happiness, both in life and death." Not a bad way to put it.

Eventually I stop loafing around and wrap myself in various layers and go outside to pick up some coffee. I'm met by an invigorating mouthful of frigid air. The day is so clear, so fresh. I run into my friend and neighbor Louise walking Sammy, her little dog. We stop and chat in front of my building as residents enter and exit, all moving quickly because of the cold. The building's claim to fame is that an Einstein look-alike lives in it. While we're speaking, our lips turning blue, this man walks by and, truly, is a dead ringer for Einstein.

"I always felt like part of me was severed"

J oan Olden is seventy-something. She has long white hair and is tall and extraordinarily slender. Each time we meet she wears something made of velvet—in royal blue, violet—and a long strand of shining pearls. Her skin is very pale. She speaks with a lacey, well-educated voice using language that's carefully phrased. She seems imperturbable both times we face each other on either side of my couch with the small tape recorder and a bowl of cashews (or other nuts or cheese) between us. Joan and her future husband, Kevin, met in September 1948 at the New York University bookshop.

"We were in psychology class together," Joan remembers. "I was in a state of euphoria. I'd just transferred from Smith College for girls, which, I felt, was such an ivory tower."

Having followed Joan to the bookstore after class, Kevin came over and asked to look at the book she was holding. She was affected by the eyes that met hers before she handed him the copy of *Look Homeward, Angel* by Thomas Wolfe.

"He looked like the pictures of Superman—fair skin, blue eyes, black hair with just the right kind of wave in it. Very, very handsome. Actually, he posed for Army, Navy and Marine posters that were made in World War II."

They were married in December 1949, then divorced in May 1963, but remarried before the year was out, only to part again four years later. She blames the divorces on extreme possessiveness and alcohol.

"I think we'd have been fine on a desert island but we ran into trouble because the real world as we knew it was full of people."

Their second split was followed by a divorce in 1980. In 2001, Joan's phone rang. Of course she recognized the voice immediately.

"The last time I even saw him was 1976, so we had almost a thirty-year gap but it didn't seem like it. He was like Rip van Winkle. He'd had a few brief contacts with his kids over the years, but had never met any of his nine grandchildren."

"You mean you picked up the phone and—just like that—it was your ex-husband after thirty years?"

"Yeah."

"Did your heart open or close when you heard his voice?"

"It was very exciting. I didn't know what he was going to look like. By then he had peripheral neuropathy and his legs clunked. He invited me to have dinner with him. We went out to Petaluma, a restaurant midtown. It happened to be the anniversary of my father's death, October 14th. He was ready to get right back together."

When Kevin and Joan first married, he was twenty-three, she was twenty. Her affluent Connecticut family and his poor, Irish Catholic family didn't mix at the small wedding or ever again.

"My mother was against the marriage but she finally agreed and at the last minute showed up at our wedding. For his mother's sake we were married in the rectory of St. Patrick's. We got the $15 wedding. The $30 wedding included music but we couldn't afford it. We had $17 for a honeymoon weekend but his mother needed carfare to get back uptown from the church with her two younger children, so we were left with $12 or $13. We went to the Tavern on the Green. They gave us champagne. How did they know we were newlyweds?"

She laughs silkily. She worked at Macy's selling ladies' underwear even though she had aspirations to be a writer; Kevin sold business forms.

"We had absolutely nothing. We got a basement apartment in Greenwich Village. Kevin was making $40 a week and helped support his mother and two younger siblings. I was going to school and working. I made about $35 a week. Of course you could buy a lot more for that in 1949."

"What did your mother have against him?"

"He was very unsure of himself socially, so the way he exhibited his feelings of inadequacy was to be rotten with everyone. He would go into a room with people and sit and read the paper. But when we were alone, he was fun and wonderfully intimate. I'd say that's the way it is today, only he's mellowed and he's on mood medication. It helps. His boiling point was so low, any little thing would make him react. You could never give someone like that a surprise party."

We laugh.

"But you married him, anyway?"

"Oh, I adored him."

Her story reminds me of one of my clippings. I pull it and ask Joan if she can relate to these lines from Lampedusa's *The Leopard*:

They were the most moving sight there, two young people in love dancing together, blind to each other's defects, deaf to the warnings of fate, deluding themselves that the whole course of their lives would be as smooth as the ballroom floor, unknowing actors set to play the parts of Juliet and Romeo by a director who had concealed the fact that the tomb and the poison were already in the script.

"And how."

Very quickly after the wedding their marriage took on a *Days of Wine and Roses* character. Kevin had started to drink heavily.

"We broke up on a number of occasions, mainly at his instigation, because his reaction is to push you away. To this day he'll say, 'I'm afraid I have to ask you to leave.' Just the same today as he did in 1948–9. I think that the reason that I get along with him now is because I still have a lot of the geisha girl in me. It never has gone away despite psychoanalysis."

An ear-splitting siren drowns out her voice, so we wait for the intrusive noise to fade.

"I thought Kevin was a diamond in the rough. I was going to make him trust me and then he would be different. I got pregnant after we were married a year. Then he left me."

"He left you while you were pregnant?"

"He was not the type when he sees you knitting booties who'll rush into your arms. He told me to take an ergot powder that women took at those times to have an abortion. While I've countenanced abortion and have helped people, it was something I personally could not live with. He left but came back two weeks later. Today he and that baby, a girl who was his spittin' image, are very close."

By the time Joan was twenty-eight she and Kevin had four children. He would leave her with no money, no food, for maybe two weeks at a time. She would call up all the YMCAs to look for him because his pattern was to register under the name O'Connor, his mother's maiden name. Then he'd come back and repent and maybe the priest would come to the house.

"I was so worried about the attractive women in his office. At the time, the *Ladies' Home Journal* said we wives should be careful because there was much temptation for a husband in the workplace, everywhere. You shouldn't let him come home to your whining, so I bought a violin and painted it pink and hung it as a decoration up on the wall with artificial ivy dripping through the strings. When Kevin would come home from work, I'd have the kids in bed by six-thirty. That meant two different meals. No help. I would put a scarf around my neck à la Isadora Duncan. I wouldn't complain about domestic problems, about how the washing machine had broken down that morning and chased me, rumbling, around the apartment. I was positive he would leave me any second because he was so handsome. I never looked at anybody else."

"Did he as far as you knew?"

"Oh, yes. When we were married about four months I discovered there was no Santa Claus. All my illusions went. I went down to his office to pick him up, I was sitting in his chair and I pulled out the drawer and there was a note lying on top that said, *You beautiful big hunk of man*. It was from someone he had, I guess, a one-night stand with when he was on a business trip to Charleston, and got drunk, as he so often did. I went rushing out of there. I was heartbroken. I don't think I have ever been so heartbroken since."

She twists the strand of pearls.

"Something altered in me when I discovered his infidelity. It was awful. I felt like I lost my innocence that night. Sex had a different flavor then. It wasn't just 'a fuck,' so I have never been the same. It was a tremendous thing for me and yet, it was really nothing. I remember . . . he'd brought me back a nightgown from Charleston. It had been so romantic. I was horrified."

At the time of the first divorce and remarriage, there were five children between ages three and ten. Joan had no money. At this point she worked in public relations. After she and Kevin divorced for the second time, she developed a crush on a woman named Dale, whom she then lived with for ten years.

"I think the idea of feeling sexual toward a woman didn't cross the boundaries of unfaithfulness. You could care about a woman. That's okay. You're not being unfaithful.

"I was thirty-eight. I encountered from this woman all the tenderness that I did not get in my marriage. Also help. Nobody had helped me. The biggest thing she ever did for me was when I came home one night . . . she lived with me and the kids at this point . . . I still remember walking in the door and seeing the laundry done and neatly stacked. No one ever did anything for me. It made me want to cry."

She stops fiddling with her pearls.

"After Dale and I stopped living together, I began living with a man. He and I lived together for seven years. I was about to marry him when I remet a childhood sweetheart who I hadn't seen in many years, Perry. Perry swept me off my feet. I sold my New York apartment and moved to St. Louis to be with him. I was there for seven years."

She tosses her long hair.

"But I was really conflicted. I couldn't get away from Dale. She was such a part of me. When my last marriage ended, I came back East. Dale was not in good shape. I have always been a caretaker. I took care of her until she died in 2000. It was shortly after she died that I remet Kevin."

Kevin had never remarried and lived in the same rent-stabilized apartment in the East Eighties. Their eldest daughter, Sharon, who had the most contact with her father through the years, had often entreated Joan to see him. Through the years Sharon's urging fell on deaf ears; too much bitter acrimony remained between them.

"What made you finally see him?" I ask.

"*La forza del destino!*" she ventures. "Actually I don't really know. It just got easier to say yes than no. My daughter's quite forceful when she wants something. It was Sharon I wanted to please. And then his call came, and I heard the word 'yes' coming out of my mouth before I even had a chance to reflect."

"When you finally met him, was it a shock?"

"Yes. His dysphoric spirit was the same"—she sighs—"and his compelling bedroom eyes . . . bad as they are . . . hadn't changed either."

When they remarried in 2001, their two daughters attended the civil ceremony. The two sons refused, because neither could forgive their father.

J oan and I speak for the second time over late afternoon drinks, also facing each other on either end of my couch. She and Kevin have been back together for three years. I bring up the subject of sex—How does sex at twenty-five compare to sex at seventy?

"Our sex life resumed *before* the wedding. When we first knew one another, I was eager but he insisted we wait until we were married. We waited the first time but not years later when we were old and gray. It's been different. . . ."

She mulls over the rest of her response to my question. I notice the first blueness of twilight. When she speaks again, she measures her words.

"In the intervening years, Kevin's put on weight. He isn't fat exactly, but is a stockier body type now. My arms don't circle him as they once did—his body feels different against mine. But then again, mine's different too. In the intervening years, I'd learned a lot about sex I didn't know when Kevin and I were young. When I had had more experience, I realized that Kevin and I always had— how can I describe it—Catholic sex. I don't think it was a Madonna complex—he's just kind of prosaic."

There's an edge of irony to her voice.

"In moments of passion I sometimes need to remind myself that it's actually Kevin. And, as for performance, sometimes it lags, but as compensation there's a tenderness, closeness, intimacy we never really had before. Now that he's gotten sicker, the sexual part of it is pretty well gone. Right before I remarried him, I had a fling with a fellow in Maine. It was my last sexual hurrah. I met this young man through one of those Internet dating things. Almost immediately we had phone sex."

"How old were you at this point?"

"Seventy. Ha, ha, ha. He was thirteen, fourteen years younger. We arranged to meet and I flew to his city, Portland. I met him at the airport. We went right to a hotel. It was amazing. I'd never been like that before. I can count on one hand the people I've slept with in my life. This guy wanted to move in with me. The sex was wonderful but I could only take him for so long. He's a man that knows no boundaries; he's the opposite of Kevin. He still faxes puzzles to me. Ha, ha."

"Can you say any more about why you remarried Kevin?"

"To tell the truth, I was in mourning for Dale. Nothing seemed to have much sense. Then, getting older, I was scared. I was slowing down. I was lonely and I knew I didn't want the fellow in Maine to move in with me. Kevin and I have a son who has a neurological disease. I think the idea of having someone to share with who would care a bit in the way I did about these kids and what was happening to them is as appealing as anything else. 'Cause I had not had that. No matter how much concern someone else felt, it's not quite the same as with the father of your child. I longed for that."

"So how else is love different in act two than in act one?"

"Well! We're speaking about love between people in their seventies with health problems. He's had heart problems, also the peripheral neuropathy. I have metastasized breast cancer. So there is a sense that time is running out. He would like me to be home all the time. Now that Kevin's really infirm, I worry about finances. The doctors told me I would have at least two good years, and I seem to be in pretty good shape. It's nothing one takes for granted. I don't worry about dying. I've never cared about living a very long time. I worry about getting things wrapped up neatly. I have some debts, credit card types, because Kevin has a very low social security and I'm not earning quite as much. I'm worried. Seems like I can never get everything tied up prettily."

"And intimacy?"

"Intimacy for us is that we do our own things but we do them together. Silence is intimate for us. We love to share books, articles; we share movies at home. Kevin's not demonstrative. After thirty years, he's forgotten how, but when it happens I'm so grateful. I feel like I'm together . . . there are no missing pieces. When I was with him in that restaurant the first time we remet, I felt like I was home. When we agreed to marry the third time, it was over double martinis. This time it was over coffee."

"How do you compare what you have now with youthful intensity?"

"I don't think physically either of us could take it. There's a time for that. Yes. He's mellowed. I don't have the most fun with him. He's not the easiest person to deal with. But, I always felt like the swan in the fairy tale, the one where the girl sews a shirt made of nettles to put over the swan who's really a prince. The girl's forced to hurry and doesn't have time to sew both sleeves. When she throws the garment over the swan, it turns back into a prince . . . but one swan wing remains. That was me. After Kevin and I parted, I always felt like part of me was severed. I never got over it. Kevin's the missing piece in my puzzle. He's the love of my life and the glue that holds me together."

"I tried everything else"

The trip from the city to High Falls, New York, in the Hudson Valley, takes about ninety minutes. Soft outlines of the Shawangunk Mountains can be seen on the horizon when I arrive in the inviting, small town. It's a short walk to the stately Arbor Bed & Breakfast. It's late afternoon on a Friday, and Bootsey, the friendly black-and-white B&B cat, sits on the railing of the front porch. The grounds have a thick coating of snow. Corinne Trang is in the kitchen preparing a meal. Corinne's fourteen-month-old daughter, Colette (who's recently taken her very first steps), is standing in the doorway holding the receiver of a cordless telephone. At various times through the interview, while the meal is being prepared, Colette talks gibberish into the phone, then—in a kind of mime—she punctuates the mock conversation with loud *ho-ho-ho's* while rocking back and forth on her heels. Though she makes us laugh we sheepishly wonder aloud, Is this what we adults look and sound like when we speak on the telephone?

"What are you making?" I ask Corinne, who is a soft-spoken, creamy, dark-haired woman.

"I'm making shrimp dumplings with a ginger-scallion cilantro dipping sauce."

Corinne and her husband, Michael, along with Colette and their little Yorkie, have been spending weekends at the Arbor while their house in the nearby woods is under construction. Corinne has published the books *Authentic Vietnamese Cooking: Food from a Family Table* (which won the Best Asian Cookbook in the English Language and Best Asian Cookbook in the World awards at the World Cookbook Fair) and *Essentials of Asian Cuisine, Fundamentals and Favorite Recipes*. The press has dubbed her the Julia Child of Asian cuisine. Corinne and her unique and renowned architect husband Michael McDonough (author of *Malaparte: A House Like Me*), whose work is collected at the Berlin Museum, Cooper-Hewitt Museum and the Corning Museum of Glass among others, call the nearby house he's designed e-House. Every Friday, while Michael and his crew work on the house, Corinne teams up with beguiling Nancy Greenwald, proprietor of the Arbor (and a fine cook in her own right), for the pleasure of preparing an unusual repast.

It's my good fortune that I've arrived on a Friday night. Tonight Nancy is acting as sous-chef. She'd been looking for a roasting pan and returns to the kitchen carrying one. While Corinne prepares, Nancy chops and assembles ingredients and contributes humor and charm to the gathering. I sit at the kitchen table admiring del-

icate Colette, watching the preparations and petting Bootsey's opulent black-and-white fur whenever he slinks by. Nancy offers me
a mug of good coffee to which I add half-and-half.

"We're also having roast duck and sticky rice," Corinne explains.

She unwraps a duck that's been thawing and reaches inside its
cavity.

"I've got to remove the offal, put the marinade inside."

Corinne was born in Paris and came to the United States when
she was eleven.

"Although my mother's French, she's been married to my father, who's Chinese, since age seventeen, and she has become es-
sentially Chinese. I come from a traditional Chinese home. As was
expected of me by my parents, I married a Chinese person, my first
husband, when I was in my twenties."

"You gave your parents what they wanted?"

Colette totters over to Corinne and Corinne sits down, takes
Colette onto her lap and lets her nurse for a few minutes.

"I gave them what they wanted. There were eight hundred fifty
people at our wedding in the United States. I wore four different
gowns."

"Eight hundred fifty people!" Nancy exclaims.

"A Chinese wedding is business. There was his side of the family, their extended family, my side. Members of my family flew in
from France and Asia. There were also a lot of my father's business
associates. Then,"—she can't help but smile—"there were five
hundred people at a second wedding in Hong Kong."

Colette's had enough and slithers off her lap, takes two tenta-
tive steps on bowlegs, then decides to crawl rather than walk.
Corinne clasps the duck in one hand and holds a small, sharp knife
in the other.

She explains, "I need to put the marinade between the skin and the meat. We're going to roast it. It's going to be different than when it's done in Indonesia, where it would have been smoking in rice husks for twelve hours. The house Michael's building has a full outdoor kitchen and grill, four burners. It also will have a dishwasher."

"Is it covered in winter?"

"Just to protect the burners."

"You can use it in the winter?"

"Yeah. Put on a coat, a hat, go right out and use the outdoor oven to make bread. Sure. It's pretty much a copy of what's going on indoors. We'll have a bread oven indoors also."

"So it's kind of a mirror image. Everything indoors and outdoors."

"Yeah. I want to teach, so I need a full kitchen. I don't need a bread oven but I just like it, it's such a romantic piece of equipment. Ancient cooking technology married to a high-tech range. We have a professional stove."

"It's interesting, the romance of this."

"Yeah. It's very romantic. Michael built it while I was pregnant with Colette. He did it with his own hands."

"That *is* romantic," Nancy comments.

"Yes. When he completed it, he put his initials and dated it on the inside."

She pulls the skin away from the duck.

"When you're roasting a meat or a chicken or bird, you don't get the flavor unless you put the marinade under the skin and over. I like bold flavors."

I'm salivating.

"You were telling me about your first marriage."

"Very quickly after I was married, I realized that it was all wrong for me, it wasn't calculated."

Colette takes hold of the telephone and rocks back and forth, laughing like a hyena. We crack up.

McDonough-Trang Family

"You left the marriage?"

"It wasn't right for me."

"And Michael?"

As if on cue, the kitchen door opens. Michael, an appealing, youthful man with an Irish face, twinkling eyes and a shock of white hair, wearing work clothes, enters the kitchen carrying a miniature Yorkie—Astérix—in his arms. Colette's face lights up and Michael bends down and hoists her up in his right arm. He's still gripping Astérix, who begins to tremble, in the crook of his left arm. It's a touching "Daddy's home" moment. He notices the tape recorder perched on the table, "Oh!"

To Michael: "I've been asking Corinne how you two met."

Corinne, rather than Michael, replies, "I was a show coordinator and my job was to manage space at the Javits Center."

Michael: "She was very corporate."

To Michael: "Tell me about who you were before you met Corinne."

"Fifteen years ago I was Alfie, the metrosexual. I made a decent amount of money as an architect and writer and was living the high life in New York. I had achieved a certain amount of professional success. I had a lot of girlfriends. I was having it all."

"You were achieving your goals?"

"Yes. It was nice. It was wine, women and song. It was *La Boheme* . . . a kind of frivolous bohemian pathway I'd chosen. I was having two- to four-year monogamous relationships, what used to be called serial monogamy in the seventies. I'd always said to myself, Ah, you're young. But, when I got into my forties, this pattern had emerged. Before I thought it was happenstance, but then I realized—no!—it was a series of failures. I thought, I want more."

"More as in what?"

"A stable relationship."

Bootsey strolls by, sees Astérix and quickly slinks away.

"So, I went to this therapist and said, 'I want to change.'"

"Male or female therapist?"

"It was a guy. He specialized in men's therapy. Robert was his name. He said, 'I want you to know you have to show up on time, keep your appointments.' So I would show up a half hour early because I was really serious. I lived way downtown; I'd be up at six to get to a seven-o'clock appointment. I kept a notebook. I was determined to change because I didn't really like who I was."

"Were you celibate while you worked on yourself?"

"I took about a year off from being with anyone."

"A conscious choice?" asks Nancy.

"Yeah. I decided to take the needle out of my arm."

Me: "Ha, ha."

"I don't want to devalue the women I was with as people . . . but . . . it just never worked out."

Colette looks up at him with wide eyes. (She's a child that never blinks.) She begins to cry, drowning out Michael's voice. He carries her over to her mother.

"I think she wants a little Corinne."

He pops Colette into Corinne's arms, and Corinne nurses her again.

"I had my notebooks, my dreams. Robert was very good. He'd say, 'Yes, this is very important for you.' And would say, 'You need to change that.' And I would go out and change it."

When Astérix begins to yelp and tremble. "Maybe he wants food too?"

He cuddles and coddles the little dog.

"I had bumped into Corinne initially when she was working at a trade fair. We met briefly."

"You glanced at her? You were introduced?"

Corinne: "He didn't look up."

We laugh.

"I was trying to sell the corporation . . ."

"He didn't even say hi."

"I wasn't that interested. She was a very attractive, capable woman. I met lots of them, quite frankly. I was probably obnoxious."

To Corinne: "Was he obnoxious?"

Michael: "That was before my therapy. I went to therapy to tone down being an asshole."

Corinne: "Didn't he say he was an asshole?"

Michael: "We bumped into each other a few months later. I was in therapy by then. She was beautiful. Intelligent. I remember thinking, 'Wow. That's the kind of girl I want.' But I'd heard she was married."

Corinne places a serving plate of dumplings in the center of the table, a small bowl filled with dipping sauce beside it. We each take a small dish. I spear a dumpling, dip it. It's scrumptious. I take another.

Michael: "Some time passed. I had a line of children's furniture made from recycled newspaper. At that point I heard that Corinne was divorced or divorcing. Part of her role was to encourage designers who were trying to do interesting things. She was very encouraging, very supportive. I said, 'Why don't you come to my studio and I'll show you more about the project.'"

Colette coos.

"I'd also heard that she had a boyfriend. I thought, It's all about stretching myself. So no touchy . . . just get to know her. So she came to my studio."

"By herself?"

"Yeah. I have a staff; there were other people around. At the time of my celibacy I dabbled with ballroom dancing. It didn't do it. Tai chi. I couldn't be bothered, it didn't have any resonance with me. I thought I might learn to cook, that it would be good for me to be more independent. Corinne and I were talking about something and cooking came up. I said, 'I really want to learn to cook Thai food. I think it's really an interesting cuisine.' I had a pretty nice kitchen in my studio. A beautiful range, a great dishwasher, a Sub-Zero refrigerator. All the fixin's. She said, 'Well, I'll teach you. We'll go shopping.' She took me to Chinatown. We started looking at food. She was a trouper. I had some cooking lessons."

Nancy uncorks a bottle of good wine.

Michael: "I was absolutely taken aback. She was like Julia Child. She knew everything and anything about cooking. And we became very, very good friends. She cooked a few meals a week for me over the next six months and she never repeated a dish, never looked at a recipe. They were classic French, Indonesian, Vietnamese. I cooked for her a couple of times from a cookbook. I had a Sicilian cookbook. I did a butterfly chicken covered with peppercorns. I did a whole Sicilian thing. Then swordfish and fresh oregano. Nothing compared to her. I was a piker."

I can't resist another dumpling.

Corinne: "I had a boyfriend. Michael and I were good friends. I think we got together every two weeks."

Michael: "There was no hanky-panky. I was very respectful of the fact that she had a boyfriend. Of course the day she broke up with him, I invited her to live with me."

Nancy and I laugh.

Corinne: "He came to my apartment at the Zeckendorf on Union Square and brought a huge bouquet of champagne-colored roses and then he took me to the museum, the Met."

Michael: "MoMA."

"I thought it was the Met?"

"No. We went to see Frida Kahlo."

"You're right."

"We did all of twentieth-century art which you can see at MoMA pretty nicely, chronologically. And then I bought her a book on Frida Kahlo I thought she'd enjoy."

"He's my pal. All of a sudden he's bringing me white roses. He didn't know that white in Chinese culture is death."

When we chuckle, Colette imitates us.

"How long did this stage go on?"

"Three weeks of officially going out. Actually, I moved in with him in November, around Thanksgiving, and then three months later we finally broke the news to my parents."

"So this was a big deal, meeting your parents?"

"To me it was going to be. Oh, my God! Number one, he's white. Number two, he's older than me. Number three, he has long hair. Three whammies."

Michael: "You should mention that my hair was long enough to be in a ponytail."

Corinne: "I'm burning the duck!"

Michael: "It's not burnt. I would say it's very crispy."

Colette begins to cry.

Corinne to Michael: "Give her the phone—that's what she wants."

He does. The crying stops and Colette resumes her mock phone conversations.

Michael: "What's curious to me is that I dated a lot of women. They didn't want me to meet their parents. It was a little bit of the *Donna Reed Show*. Here I was this middle-aged hipster who'd been all over the world, had the thousand-dollar impulse-buy down to a fine art. If I felt like going to Paris for the weekend, I would. And I had to meet Mom and Dad."

He shakes is head. Colette rolls back and forth, miming Dad.

"It was somewhere between culture shock and high hilarity but I knew it was very important to Corinne. I wanted to let them know that I was very serious . . . she comes from a very conservative background. After all, she was their only daughter. I wanted to be very respectful. I wanted to marry her. It was very serious. Very from the heart."

Me: "Even if they refused permission, were you going to do it anyway?"

Michael: "Yeah."

Me: "Afterward, did they try to undo it?"

Corinne: "Yeah. They did. He's too old for you. Forget it. It's not going to work. Then, finally, they said, 'Live together for three years and if you're still together, fine, get married.' So, three years came around."

"What sort of wedding did you have finally?"

Michael: "We wanted to have the anti-wedding. We'd both had *the* wedding. I'd been married once also, briefly. We thought, 'We don't want to get silly about this, there'll be a lot of money involved.' We said, 'What's the thing we like most in the world? What's the best thing we can imagine? The best thing is going to our favorite restaurant, being surrounded by a small group of friends and having a wonderful meal.' And that's what we did."

To Michael: "If the thirty-year-old Michael walked in and saw this Michael, what would he think of you?"

"I'll tell you something. Not Michael at thirty but Michael at sixteen or seventeen. I remember when I was in high school. Maybe fifteen. I remember reading a book. It was a French existentialist book. For the life of me I can't remember the name. At some point a younger man asks an older man, 'You've done it all. You're an artist, a writer. You've been all over the world. Here you are, you're middle-aged, you've settled down, you've got a family, kids, a mortgage. Why?' The older man answers, 'I tried everything else and I found that the greatest adventure in life was loyalty, family, responsibility. These ultimately were the most profoundly difficult, the most challenging intellectually and ultimately the most rewarding. Assuming responsibility for your own life and other people and caring for other people and being a bourgeois, this was the most existentially sublime.' I was fifteen. It stuck in my mind forever."

Nancy: "There's a shift that comes from somewhere. With me it was age. With most people I know it was age."

Me: "I agree. You've come around full circle. What about you, Corinne, as a young girl imagining your future? What would the fifteen-year-old Corinne think if she walked in right now and saw your life?"

"I don't think I would have dreamed this for myself. I wasn't really conscious then. I just followed orders."

Me: "Some couples fall in love tangoing together. You two cooked together."

Corinne: "We cook together."

"Did one of you chop? It's like a dance . . . cooking together."

"He watched me cook."

Me: "Does he eat a lot?"

Corinne: "Not just that he eats a lot—though he does eat a lot—he understands flavor. He's wonderful because he understands the architecture of food."

To Michael: "Speaking of architecture, tell me the concept of the house you're building up here in the woods?"

"It's called e-House. 'e' is intentionally ambiguous . . . electronic House . . . or environmental House. Or everything great House. The idea, as it evolved, was to take the best in building from all over the world and put it into the house. That would be in every category. Literally starting in the ground, under the ground, the best way to think of getting energy out of the ground. The best foundation. Walls. Floor finishes. Paint. Bake ovens. Kitchens. I've been an architect for twenty-five years; I've worked all over the world, done a lot of research into new building technology. There's been a tremendous explosion of building technology in the last fifteen or twenty years. Probably more so than any since the time of the Romans."

Corinne takes the duck out of the oven. We all turn to admire it.

Corinne: "We want balance in our life."

Me: "Balance?"

Simultaneously Michael says, "A way of continuing the adventure," as Corinne says, "Yes, balance."

Me: "Like the ingredients in food that balance?"

Corinne: "Yin and yang."

The dishes are assembled. The dining room table is set. Nancy stands regally at the doorway.

Me: "During the week, you're together in your studio all day long?"

Michael: "All day long. We're always together. Sometimes we travel for work. I lectured in New Zealand for a couple of weeks; she stayed home with the baby. She had to do a big tour of Asia for one of her books. I think if you love somebody you want to be with them. For us, working and living are very much the same thing. Corinne loves to cook. As an extension of that love she writes, she teaches, has a food business. I love architecture, building, I love art, as an extension of that love."

Me: "Then there's no demarcation between work and play?"

Michael: "Work is play."

Corinne smashes through the bones of the duck with a knife, dividing pieces.

Corinne: "There's no cleaver."

Michael: "We've followed our passions religiously."

Me: "That's your religion?"

Michael: "Yeah. And look where I've ended up. With a wonderful loving wife, a beautiful daughter and a little loyal Yorkie."

Corinne: "Let's eat."

Telephone in hand, Colette is put into her little seat that's attached to the table. We assemble around the Arbor's well-appointed dining room table and begin to serve ourselves. I taste the duck. Not a drop of fat. Marvelously flavorful. Crispy.

"Why is this so delicious?" I ask.

"It's the marinade," Nancy explains.

"What's in the marinade?"

"Fish sauce, galangal, lemongrass, kaffir lime leaves, ginger and sugar," Corinne replies.

Blind Love

Light the first light of evening, as in a room
In which we rest and, for small reason, think
The world imagined is the ultimate good.

This is, therefore, the intensest rendezvous.
It is in that thought that we collect sourselves,
Out of all the indifferences, into one thing:

Within a single thing, a single shawl
Wrapped tightly round us, since we are poor, a warmth,
A light, a power, the miraculous influence.

Here, now, we forget each other and ourselves.
We feel the obscurity of an order, a whole,
A knowledge, that which arranged the rendezvous.

Within its vital boundary, in the mind.
We say God and the imagination are one . . .
How high that highest candle lights the dark.

Out of this same light, out of the central mind,
We make a dwelling in the evening air,
In which being there together is enough.

—"FINAL SOLILOQUY OF THE INTERIOR PARAMOUR,"
WALLACE STEVENS

"I guess heartbreak doesn't kill that easily"

The poet Jane Mayhall, in a wheelchair, has been rolled up to the head of the long oak dining room table by a live-in nurse. A place has been cleared as the table is piled with books and papers. She's eighty-five, petite, lopsided, with melting eyes, and a complexion several shades of blushing pink roses. A place mat has been put down for her. After I'm introduced, I sit catty-cornered, on her right. I've read her recently published book of poetry—*Sleeping Late on Judgment Day*—in which various poems suggest that love doesn't die though the lover has.

> *Because we didn't believe in obligations,*
> *we never thought about divorce.*
> *And we were blessed. Going to sleep with*

you at night, to welcome the strange, uncoercive
incense of another day.

— FROM "NOTES FOR A SIXTIETH WEDDING ANNIVERSARY"

Seeing a snapshot of you,
I thought your hands were my hands.

— FROM "THE SUPERSTITION"

Jane's words underscore her belief that regardless of grief and ill health, curiosity and honoring of life go on:

My heart is bursting with homage as I
head off to a hostile eternity

— FROM "TOO MUCH IS NOT ENOUGH"

These ideas—sorrow and hope folded together—are what has brought me to the West Sixties and has given me the courage to trouble a very ill woman in the endgame of her life. Part II in Jane's new book, the section titled *Love Poems*, repeatedly eulogizes the vivid passion and continuity of a love that began in the thirties and sustained itself into the new millennium. Now, however, there's the cloud of heartbreak that Jane has lived beneath since the death in 1997 of the source of this intense passion, her husband of sixty years, the Baltimore-born writer and publisher Leslie Katz.

As soon as I'm sitting in her living room, the line from "Notes for a Sixtieth Wedding Anniversary"—*love is private*—comes to mind, rendering me tongue-tied. Her poems make mention of the many objects belonging to Leslie that remain in the apartment. His coat hangers still hang in the closet. His comb lies on the dresser. Every corner of the lofty sitting/dining area with twenty-foot ceilings is crammed with expensive books and objects, and very good art. One of the distinctive things about that room is that it is filled with the effects of Leslie Katz's work. He was a fine editor and writer who also had an extraordinary eye for photographic images, particularly American ones. Unless you have seen his books (which are collectors' items, of course) it is hard to describe how extraordinary Leslie Katz's work is. He was deeply connected to Berenice Abbot, Walker Evans, Lee Atwater, among many others. Around us, back, front and center, are Leslie's books.

I ask Jane, "Do you ever feel, in your grief, that you want your husband's things away from you? Or do you want them around you?"

"I always want them around me. I want the books he published—Eakins Press—all around me. In fact, I wish he were back all the time. In fact I wake up sometimes in the middle of the night and I think he's just across the room . . . sitting across the room."

"How does that feel? Is it comforting? Or?"

"It's just normal."

"What do you think Leslie would have had to say about your new book? Was he a tough critic or easy?"

"He was not hard but he was specific. He would never say a thing was good if it wasn't good. We were alike in this understanding."

"Did he know any of the poems in the book or were they all written after his death?"

"All were written after."

"So, if he were here he would methodically go through each poem and give his thoughts?"

"He would say, 'This is that.' He was always kind, never taking over."

"Can you think of which poems he would have responded to?"

"I think he wouldn't have liked the death poems."

"May I ask when you first met Leslie Katz?"

"I can't remember the specific year. It was at Black Mountain College, my first year, his second year, and it was about 1935. Something like that. I thought he was very good looking."

"How old were you?"

"About sixteen."

"Wow."

"He was sixteen too . . . three months under."

"Going to college that young, you must have been geniuses."

"No we weren't."

"Do you remember the first things you spoke about?"

"We were like brother and sister. The first thing he showed me was the picture of his girlfriend. He was proud of her and he wanted me to know that he knew people who looked like that."

"You became friends?"

"We became intellectual friends. We also had a kind of brother-sister thing that stayed with us all these years. We grew up together. We read the same books, had the same ideas, there was a sameness about us. We both were very erotic. We tried to go to the same classes."

"Did you study music in college?"

"Yes. I played the piano. He played the trombone, which I thought was too unglamorous. I told him he should play the flute. He immediately went out and got his father to buy him a flute."

"Did he learn to play?"

"He took lessons in Asheville, North Carolina."

"Did you play flute and piano together?"

"No, we didn't, but politically we stood together."

"Did you have any sense that you were two halves of a whole that had been divided?"

"We must have been because we immediately depended on each other."

Jane's caregiver brings several medications that need to be taken before lunch. Besides eulogizing Leslie, there are poems in *Sleeping Late* that pay tribute to their many prominent friends—Lincoln Kirstein, James Still, Theodore Roethke. I'd been told that the way she and Leslie dealt with the differences of their religions—he was Jewish, she Baptist—was to convert to the other's religion. The caregiver brings the tray containing her lunch of chicken and green beans to the table, and I stop asking questions so that she can eat. The hand that picks up the fork is swollen.

"I'll turn off the tape recorder?"

"Don't. I want to take advantage of your being here. I always felt so much at home with Leslie."

"This is why I want to hear what you have to say, someone who managed to have a lifelong relationship as you and Leslie did. How does love change with time? How does love not change with time? Tell me more about the beginning."

"We lived together at Black Mountain. Our whole romance took place at Black Mountain. We'd rather talk about philosophy than make love. Leslie had a car. We drove, we'd take the records of Stravinsky. We'd listen to Stravinsky and that was more meaningful than making love. We were slow in coming to the act of love."

"After Black Mountain, did you go away together?"

"I went to take care of my mother. Leslie drove up to Louisville to see me in his car. The thing got very complicated because the head of Black Mountain, who was John Rice, the man who started the whole idea of students teaching the teachers—it was really carried to an exaggerated point—John Rice fell in love with me and Leslie was madly in love with John Rice because he was a big brain. John Rice wanted me to make love. He wrote a song about me, the glamour girl of Black Mountain College: *'Cause I have such a beautiful brain, I set all the boys afurl with my mind and knowledge. I had such a beautiful brain. I was the glamour girl of Black Mountain College.* They wanted me to leave because I was being immoral, when all I did was hold John Rice's hand. I had no physical relationship with him at all."

"Incredible."

"Yes, it was incredible, and, as you can see, I'm still boasting about it."

"Was there room in your relationship to love other people?"

She hasn't touched her food.

"There was room. We were proud of it. We made a lesson of it, of being free, free of each other."

"Did this stay true for sixty years?"

"From beginning to end we wanted always to be free for other people and we'd always come back to each other—from all our adventures—it was worse than the flapper age, trying to live up to some philosophy. I never thought of that."

"You always told each other the truth no matter how difficult it might be?"

"We made a habit of it because we always felt at home with each other. This brother-sister thing is very important. In New York, I taught at the New School. Nothing seemed to follow Black Mountain but the New School."

"I went to the New School too. When Leslie became ill, were you prepared in any way for sickness?"

LOVE IN THE SECOND ACT   *115*

"No. He had Parkinson's. He said, 'Why did this have to happen to me?' I didn't think it would end in tragedy though."

"You didn't have a sense of mortality, that either of you might outlive the other?"

"No."

"Were you solitary people in the last twenty years that you were together? Were you alone a lot? Or, were you often with friends?"

"We drank a lot. We lived in a paradise of drinking."

"A lifelong paradise or did you have to moderate?"

"No. We didn't have to moderate."

"Do you still drink?"

"I don't want to. My doctor thinks I should. He says I should end it all gloriously but I don't want to do it that way. Not like we did long ago. Long ago when we visited Conrad Aiken, he'd serve such big drinks I'd pour mine on the houseplants and his wife would say about the dying plant, 'I really don't know what's happening with this plant.'"

She titters.

"They were martinis which Conrad called martoonis."

"Cole Porterish."

"We had a paradise life."

"Do you feel that some of the poems are able to express well the echo of this rich life?"

"Tragically, yes. It brings me always to the tragedy."

"Are you writing right now?"

"Prose. Right now I'm reading stories."

She puzzles.

"I can't remember the name of the writer. He's one of those British writers who is half Irish, half British, half Welsh. My father was Welsh. He was a postal telegrapher in Louisville, Kentucky. Now I've gotten proud of him. Leslie thought he was rescuing me from poverty. His father was a businessman. We lived in a poor neighborhood but when a seller came by selling great books—Harvard Classics—my father bought them and read me Dostoyevsky when I had a toothache. *Crime and Punishment.*"

"I'm jealous."

"I'm jealous too. My father was so ashamed of living in a tough neighborhood a few blocks from the Standard Oil Company."

"Where did your father get his love of literature?"

"I think from his aunt."

"It's sort of like a torch that's passed from person to person."

"I was so aware of that. I think if ever my work amounts to anything it was because of those old ladies who were so proper . . . those old Southern ladies."

"Did you ever teach in the South?"

"I taught in Kentucky. James Still was one of my heroes. I met him at Yaddo. I'm jumping around a lot."

"I don't mind."

"James Still is practically self-taught. He was a mountain boy. I always had this brother-sister relationship with men."

"Were you ever drawn to men who were different . . . opposite? . . ."

"Not tough ones."

"You had one taste in the kind of men you liked for your entire life?"

"That's true. I don't think Leslie would have liked the death poems. I think he wouldn't have wanted me to leave the impression of death anywhere."

"If he outlived you, do you think he would have been able to cope without you?"

"No. He was very pro men. Lincoln Kirstein was one of his dearest friends. Lincoln thought they were meant for each other. Leslie was not gay, he was very close to the edge of being very close to men."

"So, if he had outlived you, you think he would have had supportive men around him?"

"He might not have. I think he might just have died of heartbreak. Probably. I never thought of that."

"I guess heartbreak doesn't kill some people that easily . . . if only one could physically die."

"That goes on in my mind all the time."

"Was there ever a point that you and Leslie thought you wouldn't make it . . . to go on together, when you thought of terminating your partnership?"

"No. Our ideas were so luxurious. He wanted me to read Wallace Stevens to him when he had Parkinson's."

I think of "Final Soliloquy of the Interior Paramour." I ask Jane if it was one of the poems she read to Leslie. I say the last lines— *We make a dwelling in the evening air / In which being there together is enough*—and ask if she and Leslie had a particular Wallace Stevens poem.

"I can't think of a single one now. Death . . . grief . . . and truth are gross. . . ."

She seems to be searching for words she can't find. Finally she says, "It is the actuality that I can't stand his being gone. I can't stand his being gone. I see it as a great oppression. Leslie had these ideas. He was the son of a businessman and he was . . . we were always right in a certain way. The two of us were always right. A lot of people graced the funeral. Do you know Lee Friedlander? He was a friend of Walker Evans . . . in fact he was about the best photographer Walker Evans ever knew outside of himself. He said in the tribute to Leslie—when he described Leslie's spirit—he said, 'It was granite.' He said, 'He was so strong, he was granite.' "

Jane Mayhall

"What would you say your spirit is, put in terms of a stone or a material substance?"

"Wishy-washy. I'm dying. I mean I'm dying in a way. I mean I'm not going to be a pretty sight because I don't have . . ." She stops and lowers her eyelids, then continues, "Leslie had a strong nature. I wish I did but I don't. I'm anti-death right now. I hope I don't make death sound so trivial. Everybody looks at it differently. My friends think I'm a coward."

"Do you think you're a coward?"

"Yes. I'm no good without him. I'm writing short stories because I must be looking for a replacement . . . a way to say it is vile. I know perfectly well that nothing can replace him."

*"It was like oysters. When you eat oysters
and get sick and try them again. I knew
he would always be my oyster."*

We sit on my south-facing enclosed terrace so she can smoke, letting black tea brew in the pot because she likes it strong. A small electric heater augments the central heating that doesn't always reach from the living room onto the terrace.

"Is being in love different for you as you approach fifty or has it stayed the same?" I ask Chantal "Tessa" Dahl, daughter of the writer Roald Dahl and the Academy Award–winning actress Patricia Neal.

"For me it's been the same. In fact I was as much in love with one particular man in my forties as I was when I was fifteen."

"Oh?"

Tessa's a fine and acknowledged writer, having published a novel and a multitude of magazine pieces. She admires the Greek Church framed by the snow-covered rooftops of Chelsea below us. She's six feet tall, statuesque, and as beautiful as her mother was in her prime. Her life has been tempestuous to say the least. She was raised in England, has been married twice, has four children, and has had innumerable love affairs, many with famous men. At the moment she's between relationships and has rented an apartment on the East Side of Manhattan near her mother. She lights a cigarette. When I lift the teapot she sloughs me off, gesturing that it needs more time to steep, then asks if my recorder is on. When I nod, she shakes out the lit match and begins speaking in an educated English accent.

"When I was fifteen, I saw a motion picture with the actor David Hemmings. He was a big star at the time—he'd just made *Blow-Up* with Vanessa Redgrave. He was just about to do *Charge of the Light Brigade*. I took one look at him and wanted him. When I got into my bed that night I said, 'God, if you give me anything in my life, please give me David Hemmings.' A few months later, my mother somehow had me cast in a movie that was being made in Nova Scotia. We went off and made it, and one of the talk shows invited my mother and me on."

"In England?"

"In England when we got back. The other guest star on the talk show happened to be David Hemmings. So we met, and soon met again at what was then a trendy club—Tramps. He was the first person who ever kissed me. On the dance floor at Tramps. He was married. I was convinced that he was going to leave his wife and come to me. I would leave school and take presents to his agent to give to him. I'd arrange to have lunch with him and he'd send his agent and not himself. It was really an unrequited love."

She decides the tea has steeped long enough and fills our cups, adds milk.

"One day I was having lunch with my mother and father, and David was sitting nearby and it set my heart hammering. When I was nineteen, I ran into him at a nightclub, and that started a huge love affair. I was *so* in love with him. I was *beyond* in love with him. It was a strange mixture of infatuation and love. I thought, This time he'll marry me. But, one night he took me out to dinner and told me he was getting married, and it was not to me."

Tessa puts out her cigarette.

"The next day I saw a newspaper headline that said, Movie Star Weds in Secret. I'd been convinced if I could get him into my bedroom, he'd change his mind, but I'd been wrong. Cut to years later. He always stayed in touch with me. He'd send me postcards, little things. I'd have a lover or a husband. David's wife became a close friend of mine. She and I would have heart-to-hearts. She'd say, 'Never marry an alcoholic.' And I went on being in love with him. I even had an affair with another actor who looked terribly like him, a poor man's version of David. Eventually—years later—someone told me that David and his wife were getting divorced. I had a boyfriend at that point. I said—'So what?' Pretending I didn't care."

She stirs her tea.

"Then, someone else told me he was in London and where he was staying and why didn't I call him. Straight away I called him. He was thrilled to hear my voice. He was overjoyed. He invited me for a drink that night. It was an amazing night. He was late but I stayed and waited."

"How late?"

"He must have kept me waiting about forty-five minutes. It was all right being stood up when I was seventeen but not all right when I was in my forties. But . . . he finally came in and was divine to everyone, particularly divine to me. This began an amazing love affair, a love affair of such proportions."

She sips tea, takes another cigarette out of its package.

"Soon afterward he invited me to Budapest where he was making a movie. I arrived and didn't realize that he'd kicked out a woman for me, rather like a dog. I would have forgiven him anything. Eventually he asked me to marry him. I thought, This is it. We will get married. We *will* get married. Nothing in the world would ever mean as much to me as David. We went back to England and did a lot of interviews together. We spoke to the magazines—the best tabloids— *Hello!* magazine. I just was so addictively in love with him. It was an extraordinary time of my life. All the agonies, the waiting and waiting, wanting and wanting—suddenly there he was and he was mine."

She empties her teacup and pours another.

"His drinking was getting out of control that year. We did an intervention. He said he'd go to Hazelden, the alcohol rehab in Minnesota. But he said he'd go only if I went with him. He just wouldn't go without me. So I went. We didn't realize until we got there that the men and women were put in separate wings. We'd have these secret trysts. We'd have a tryst in the woods. It was summer and when we were making love in the woods we were slapping our sides the whole time. Mosquitoes—the national insect of Minnesota."

I've been to Minnesota and she'd hit the nail on the head.

"One of the most agonizing parts of it: I'd given him a plush terry-cloth bathrobe to wear at Hazelden. After we'd been there nearly a month, a woman who was working at Hazelden brought it to me and said, 'This is closure. He's going back to his wife,' and handed me the bathrobe. 'You've got to leave before he does—it's psychologically important. However, we want you to come back and deal with your issues of love addiction.'"

"Ha, ha."

"I left and I booked this family holiday in Naples, Florida, at the Ritz-Carlton. When my family and I arrived, they were taking down the chandeliers, removing paintings. Suddenly they announced on the loudspeaker that there was a hurricane coming, Hurricane Andrew. They wanted us all to leave but we had nowhere to go. That was the night David was leaving . . . really, really leaving me for good and I knew it. Sophie, my daughter, and I went for a walk on the beach. It was that absolute lull before a storm . . . that quiet. Nothing moved. There were searchlights from the balconies. The damage the hurricane was going to do was ahead. It was very, very fitting. It was a sort of metaphor for what happened with that relationship. A huge hurricane went through and off it went. David went back to his wife."

She smokes her cigarette. It seems as though she's finished speaking but then continues.

"He did come back three years later. He asked me again if he could come back and I said no."

She puts the cigarette in the ashtray, cradles her teacup in both hands.

"I felt it was like oysters. When you eat oysters and get sick and try them again. I knew that he would always be my oyster. That was the end of

Tessa and David

our love affair. When he died two years ago, I really grieved. He was definitely the love of my life. I never thought he'd be the love of *all* of my life—through everything—from the age of sixteen. He just died and my love went on and that's the end."

"You've got to see it to the end"

At some point, when I'd commented on the blind love for David Hemmings that lasted so many years, Tessa Dahl had quipped, "You should speak with my mother. She'll have a thing or two to say about immutable love. Ask her about Gary Cooper." I told her I would do just that, and she offered to speak with her mother and set up a meeeting. True to her word, before too many days have passed, an appointment was set up.

On my way to see Tessa's mother, I promise myself never again to take the crosstown bus. It's a sleety day at three in the afternoon, the time that all the children on the East Side are getting out of school and squeezing into the buses. Between stuffed backpacks, soppy umbrellas, shopping bags, fogged-up windows, winter coats and pent-up irritability, it's not a pleasant trip. Tessa's Academy Award–winning mother is actress Patricia Neal. (*Breakfast at Tiffany's, Hud, The Fountainhead* with Gary Cooper, *The Subject Was Roses, Cookie's Fortune,* and so on.) Her apartment is on the East River. Even though the bus takes forever, I'm early, so I walk to a railing above the river and watch several freight barges glide gently toward the Fifty-ninth Street Bridge past chunks of ice. Then I take the elevator upstairs.

When coat and scarf are taken by an assistant (I'm told to call her "young friend"), I'm escorted to a large round table where, surrounded by photographs in polished silver frames, the actress sits on a silk-covered Chippendale chair. The room has large picture windows that frame the leaden river and its ice floe islands. That view is the backdrop to our conversation. Patricia's young friend asks us each what we'd like to drink and we both request tea. Small talk is made. Finally, I tell her I'm turning on my tape recorder.

"I won't say anything dirty," she promises in a vibrant theatrical voice.

I give a little thumbnail description of the book, including the title.

"That's a pretty good title," she remarks.

"Any comments on what the second half of your life's been like . . . in the area of love?"

She laughs merrily. I can see why people love her.

"Gary Cooper was my great love."

"You're somebody who's been to the heights and you've been to the depths."

"I've been in all those places."

"How do you find life at this point?"

"It's very good. My walk is not perfect. I'm quite forgetful. I can't see out of the side of this eye. My stroke killed that. It was terrible. But I'm living my life to the full right now."

Patricia Neal

Her friend brings a tray with mugs of tea, cream, and sugar. I ask if she knows the Fitzgerald quote about American lives.

"I didn't know he said that."

"The idea that we get only one chance and that's it."

"I've fouled up a lot of mine."

"What do you enjoy most at this point in life?"

"I like people paying attention to me. Ha, ha, ha. I love it. I say, Oh thank you, thank you, thank you. No. I have a house in Martha's Vineyard. It's a great house. It was built by the captain of the ship of someone connected to *Moby-Dick* and it's good. I love it. I spend from April, May, almost June until October."

The young woman asks for some letters that had just been signed. While she rummages for them, my eyes drift to the flowing river. I see the sleety rain has turned sluggish, that fat wet snowflakes are sticking to the corners of the large picture window-panes. When she speaks again, her voice has switched gears, from theatrical to lilting, with a slight Southern edge to it.

"I know a lot about love. It's all stayed right here in my heart." She touches her bosom.

"Can you say more about this? You mean you've had plenty of romantic love?"

"Much much much too much. I was with a lot of small loves. Then I went with Gary Cooper who I loved."

Neal and Cooper starred in *The Fountainhead*. (Gary Cooper portrayed Howard Roark, who at one point says, while hoisting Patricia Neal, playing Dominique Francon, up in his arms and carries her toward the bed to the swelling accompaniment of Max Steiner music in the background, "I loved you from the first moment I saw you and you knew it.") She describes how Cooper was the kind of man who exuded trust, confidence, protection. As soon as people met him, within ten minutes they'd feel as if he'd been their friend for years.

"I went with him for five and a half years. Anyway, he's my love still. I will always love him. When we were clearly broken up, I went to New York and had very little money. Really very little. I moved into a tiny apartment. I did *Another Part of the Forest*, Lillian Hellman's play. I loved doing it. But anyway . . . where am I?"

"You're in your first play. It seemed to come easily."

"The first play was lovely. I met Ro-al-d Dahl, at Lillian Hellman's house." She draws his name out into three distinct syllables.

"He looked so fascinating. I sat next to him at supper. I hated him at the end of supper. . . . He paid no attention to me. The whole time he was talking to Leonard Bernstein. Then he called me up about two days later, asked me out for a date and I said I couldn't go. He called me again two days later. I couldn't think of an excuse. So I went."

A long, low barge carrying mounds of freight that are covered with black tarps slowly passes across what's left of the view of the river as the fat, wet snowflakes cover the glass.

"Now look at the boats. Aren't they great?"

"Oh, my!"

"It's just fabulous what I see living here."

"Yes. It's fantastic."

Her laughter is infectious though I don't know why we're laughing; we laugh together like old friends.

"But . . . so I went out with him. Then he asked me to marry him some months later and I did. I didn't want to. I said no. No. But finally I did, and, anyway, I'm not going to go into that."

Again there's a distraction; when she turns her attention back to me, she asks with a regal tone, "What was I talking about?"

"You were talking about the men in your life."

"As I told you, Gary Cooper. That's the one who I loved and who I still love."

"He must have been quite a bit older than you."

"Yes, he was. He was born in 1901. I was born in 1926. He was twenty-five years older than me."

Cooper was six feet three inches, Neal is at least six feet. Both tall. Him—soft-spoken, lean. Her—forceful, sultry. Both sexy as hell. They must have made quite a couple.

"So you feel you've had a great love in your life and that's enough?"

"I have. It's quite enough. People seem to be greedy about this. Oh, yes. God, I know people who get married five, six, seven, eight times. I cannot imagine doing that. I've had five children. One who sadly died. But I have four left and they're lovely. One lives in Florida. One lives in Boston. One lives in California. One lives in New York, with me, and it's very good. Tessa. She doesn't live with me at my house but she lives near."

"And grandchildren?"

"I have . . . interesting that you're asking . . . because I have four granddaughters and two grandsons and I'm happy to tell you that my son's wife is pr-eg-n-ant, and they've been married nine years."

"This will be the first child your son has?"

"I'm very happy. Isn't that good?"

"Yes."

"I love it."

"You've built a dynasty."

She laughs.

"Not really. There are people with a lot more than me."

"And you're about to go for Thanksgiving with your family to Martha's Vineyard?"

"Yes. Tessa and I . . . we are going."

The phone rings. "I'll see who this is."

I turn off the tape recorder and once more my eyes are drawn over to gaze at the river but the lacy glaze of snow has obscured the view; it's as if we're sealed inside the room. The tea is delicious; it's milky and tasty. Patricia Neal finishes her phone call and hangs up.

"Is there anything you haven't done in your life that you'd like to do?"

"I can't think of anything. I'm very sorry that I had my stroke. I'd just won the Oscar. I was ready to go and I had a terrible stroke. I mean, everybody was so divine to me."

"You must appreciate life very much . . . you came so close to losing your own?"

"Listen, baby, when I came to, when I could think at all, I was gaga. I don't know how many months it was. It was impossible. You have no idea. I couldn't talk. I got everything wrong. But then when I began to get a little better, I hated life in the beginning, I really hated it. But then I started working with Valerie Eaton-Griffith, who began therapy with me, and I adored her and so life became good and I've been happy ever since."

"So you've relished life?"

"Many times I could have killed myself but I love life really."

"And you have no regrets in your life?"

"Oh, sure."

"Or is that too personal?"

"I'm very sorry that I lost Roald. Felicia took him away from me. I like her now. We're friendly in fact. At the end of it I made up with them because I was so tired of hating them. Ha, ha. Theo was having a party . . . thirtieth birthday."

"Theo is your son?"

"Yes, my son. I wrote them a letter and I said, It's time for me to give up the hate. I'd love to come to Theo's birthday party. Oh, they were so happy. So I went and Roald came to see me where I was staying. He was so happy to see me and he embraced me. It's been good ever since. That was in July or August and he died in November."

"So you'd made peace?"

"We *had* made peace."

"It's wonderful."

"If I hadn't made peace, I don't know what I would have done."

As I swallow the last drop of milky tea, I notice that my white mug is embossed with a painting of a good-looking cowboy in a cowboy hat with a smart neckerchief tied around his throat. On the mug is written: Gary Cooper. She notices too.

Wistfully she tells me, "He died of cancer. He was sixty. He died a week after his sixtieth birthday."

"Any advice for people who feel that life isn't worth it or that the world is too miserable?"

"Chin up. That's all I can say. Life is tough. Very tough. You just can't give up. I know people who've killed themselves. Silly. Pretty silly. You've got to see it to the end."

"See it to the end."

"Till the curtain falls."

"Till the curtain falls."

She laughs.

"That's it."

"There was no before"

In the living room of my parents' apartment near Washington Square, my mother sits on *her* chair, the one with a pile of magazines (like O—*The Oprah Magazine*, *Vogue*, *The New Yorker*) beside it. She's eighty-five, has a clear mind but, tragically, very bad health. Over the course of our conversation, I'm surprised at how many new bits and pieces of information she tells me that I hadn't known before.

"Exactly how long have you been married?" I ask.

"We've been married sixty-four years."

I explain that I'd like to know how love changes over a lifetime. How she and my father have changed. If love has been immutable. How they've sustained a relationship over so many decades.

"We've defied the odds, that through thick and thin and up and down, we're here. We've weathered all that."

"Right."

"And we've grown up along the way. We met in college. We married soon after and lived happily ever after with the usual ups and downs of a pre–World War Two wedding."

"Was it unusual to marry quickly in those days?"

"It was because of the war. The war was coming and we were impatient."

"How many months did you date?"

"Three months. We were both finishing college, Brooklyn College. Daddy courted me during Easter vacation. My parents and sisters were away on vacation, he came to my house every day for lunch and my Little Grandmother made mashed potatoes every day because she knew Daddy liked her mashed potatoes. She was my mother's mother. We called her Little Grandma."

"Perhaps she was luring him into the family. How old were you?"

"Twenty."

"Do you remember where you went on your first date?"

"Sure. We visited with friends and then decided to go to a late movie at the Brooklyn Paramount. They used to have a midnight show. It had snowed heavily that day but we went. We saw *Strawberry Blonde*, which was romantic too. We loved that movie."

"Have you seen it since?"

"Sure. When we see it we get the sentimental feeling. Then we came out at two o'clock in the morning. Daddy brought me home, then he had to walk all the way to his home because all the buses stopped running . . . several miles."

"Had you been dating anyone else?"

"Oh, sure."

"Did you just drop them?"

"Sure."

"Was it love at first sight?"

"It was fast."

"He didn't have to chase you or you him?"

"No. But his folks expected him to go out and work and bring money back to the family, so they weren't that happy."

"Did you go to his home?"

"I came for Friday night supper and his mother cooked and cooked and cooked. She made a full Friday night dinner with gefilte fish and soup and chicken. The whole works."

My mother's hair remains partially dark; it's cut in a neat, neck-length style. As usual, she's wearing something chic and casual.

"Can you remember the first time you noticed him?"

"I'll tell you. It was at a party given by our Eco Club. I started college as a science major, had physics, physiology, but later I became an eco major."

"Can you explain what attracted you to the subject?"

I'd meant economics but she took it to mean Daddy.

"I'll tell you. At the Christmas party, each person entertained and when Daddy got up, he buttoned his jacket and sang "Sam, You Made the Pants Too Long." I decided he was good-looking, he could sing."

"In his tenor voice?"

"He has a gorgeous tenor voice. Then we all went to Coney Island and had hot dogs at Nathan's."

I'm startled. I've always remembered the story told differently, that they had first met when he helped her pick up a typewriter or calculator in a statistics class.

"Describe your wedding."

"It was a simple wedding, I wore a blue dress and a blue hat to match. I still have the hat and the dress in the closet. Didn't I ever show you?"

Of course I'd seen it a million times.

"My veil is folded up too . . . a chin-length veil . . . it was a dress with a coat. I've saved the little bride and groom that stood at the top of the cake too."

"What was the date?"

"May 15, 1941, a school day."

"You got married on a school day!"

"That day I went to school and had a test in economics. I got a very good mark. That night we honeymooned in the St. George Hotel which was a local hotel in Brooklyn. The next day we went to school. Then we lived with my folks. At that point my grandparents moved next door to my aunt's place. We all lived in one house next to the other. Soon thereafter we got an apartment of our own on Crown Street in Brooklyn, a one bedroom. I made my own bedspread, made a lot for that place. We graduated, and Daddy got a job at Martin's Department Store on Fulton Street, setting up perpetual inventory for the store. He made $15 a week. They raised it to $18 but then he quit that job and spent the whole summer looking for work. Before the war it was hard. The war started December 7th. We knew our lives would be different."

There's gravity in her voice.

"Right after your brother Teddy was born your father got drafted and was sent away to training camp. Since his salary was going to be $15 a month, we put our furniture in storage and I moved back to my folks."

I had never known this.

"It must have been a difficult time."

"Very difficult time. He was injured shortly thereafter in a train-ing accident and so I would go by train all the way to Cape Cod to visit him in the Army hospital where he was. And then he was dis-charged. I can still see him walking down the street in his uniform with his kit bag over his shoulder."

"Did you know he was coming?"

"No. I spotted him coming down the street. The Veterans Ad-ministration helped him get a job at the National Bureau of Eco-nomic Research. He borrowed $100 from Aunt Dorothy and went to graduate school."

"Throughout your entire sixty-four-year marriage you both have loved theater, movies. . . ."

"I think every movie and every play we saw was a highlight. One of the jobs he had early on, and he had many jobs, was as a theater manager in a movie house on Forty-second Street. This was the one that showed foreign films, and, at that time, most of the foreign films came from Great Britain. So we saw wonderful movies. Early on we had a subscription to a host of modern dance performances at a high school in Manhattan, the Needle Trades High School. We loved to dance. He was a good dancer. That was another requirement, he had to be a good dancer."

"So he could sing and he could dance and he was funny?"

"No. He wasn't funny."

This astonishes me since I've always thought of my father as funny, very funny.

"Did you think, in the beginning, you would have imagined . . ."

"What my life . . . ? No. I had no notion and I had no preconceived idea what I wanted. We made it up as we went along."

"Have you found life harder than you thought?"

"Just different."

"Why do you think you were able to do what so many couples were not?"

She clears her throat; chokes. When she stops, she says, "We took 'for better or for worse' very seriously. We didn't think we had choices. If we had differences, we thrashed them out."

"Right."

"I think the essence of a whole lifetime is that we took for granted that we'd stay together."

"So it was an absolute, unshakable commitment that you made and kept?"

"Yes, and we had hard times and good times."

"Does it seem like a long time that you've been together?"

"It seems like forever. There was no before."

. . .

A few weeks later I sit in the living room with both my father and my mother.

I say to my father, "When I asked Mother how you met, she said you were in a college club together, she heard you singing "Sam, You Made the Pants Too Long."

"That was later. Actually we were in the same class and she was sitting in front of me and she looked terrific from behind and then when she got up at the end of class, I saw that she was terrific. So thereafter, for the next few weeks, she and I walked in the same direction. I walked in a direction opposite from the one I wanted, but I walked her to the subway, the IRT."

That's the story we'd always heard before.

"So you finally asked her out?"

"In February or thereabouts, I began to date her."

"He really asked me out on the day of my birthday."

"See, I don't remember that."

"You came to my house and my mother had a cake on the table and she lined up all my birthday cards and you had never had a birthday cake."

"Right, right. An interesting thing was when I saw that birthday cake and everything else, I had never had a birthday party, I told Mommy—Shirley—when we are married, every birthday we're going to run for seven days."

"Eight days. From Sunday before to Sunday after."

To my father: "What kinds of things did you do when you went out?"

My mother replies: "We went rowing in Prospect Park. We went for walks. He had no money."

"I didn't have much money. I used to carry change in my pocket and I could count it with my hand to know exactly how much money I had and if we could go in for a soda or something. Don't kid yourself, you know, that was a very serious problem."

My father's glasses are perched on top of his crew cut. He's got hazel eyes, long fingers that have become deformed by arthritis. The nails have become so hard they're almost impossible to cut.

"I was twenty; she was twenty-one, a few months older. When we got married, everybody said she was pregnant and everyone stood around and counted months. They thought I had to marry her. Then, when Teddy was born on the twentieth month. . . ."

My mother's look says, Enough! He stops speaking. My mother explains, "His mother and father had to go with him to get the license. The age was twenty-one."

To my father: "What do you attribute the fact that you've stuck together?"

"All differences"—he chortles—"were trivial and we resolved those. And there's another thing, ninety-nine percent of the confrontations . . . I always conceded that she was right."

To my mother: "So if the twenty-one-year-old Shirley came in now, would she approve of the life you've made? What would she have to say about the eighty-five-year-old Shirley?"

"That's a good question. I could see ways it could have been better. I can see ways it could have been worse."

"You had something higher than the last argument, any argument. . . ."

"Oh, yeah."

"You had vows and you believed them?"

"It wasn't vows. It was important that you solved the differences."

"All right," and to my father, "What about the twenty-year-old you, what would he have to say to the eighty-four-year-old?"

"I have had immeasurable affection, love for her, every minute that we're married. It never in any way deviated from that. The only thing that ever bothered me was once we went to a party, her twenty-fifth high school anniversary, and while we were there, a fellow came running across the hall. He says, 'I've been looking for you, Shirley.' I was very uncomfortable with the fact that anyone else was looking for her . . . wanted her."

I look at my mother. Her face is unreadable.

He adds, "I think the most significant thing is . . . in the course of a day, many—you call them arguments—misunderstandings, but I never viewed any one of them as significant, so I never would argue strongly for it. Yeah. Have it your way. Who the hell cares."

I can see my mother's ire rising.

"That's not true. When I decided I wanted to go to work, I had to convince you."

"Oh, yes . . . that's an exception."

"It was a running argument. I stood in the middle of the street and was never going to go home again."

"I don't remember that."

"I wanted to work."

"I'll tell you what happened. I was teaching in college at this point. I came home in 1950. I had just been given tenure. I came home. I felt terrific because I'd taught there five years. She said, 'What are you making? Your salary?' I said, 'I got a raise to $2,000.'"

Me: "A year?"

He nods.

"She said, 'You're no . . .'"

She finishes his sentence, ". . . prince."

Me: "Would you like to take that back now?"

"No."

"Another word she used, a worse one. She said, 'I guess I'll have to go to work.' We had three children already. The fact of the matter was that though I didn't want her to work, she guessed correctly that, as a college professor, no matter how it increased it would be a very low level of living. So she went to work. She went to work to make money. Not for glory."

"I realized, I had the same education he did. Why shouldn't I have a professional life too?"

"And not only did she have a professional life, while she was working she went back and got the Ph.D. A tremendous achievement on her part. In the meantime, she always cooked meals."

"Nobody ever cooked but me. But he was very helpful. We marketed together. We fixed the house together."

"We did . . . do everything together."

Me: "So you were and are a good team?"

My mother quickly responds, "Oh yeah."

My father adds with pride, "Until this year we were seeing fifty plays and dance recitals a year."

"But there was a period when we were lucky if we saw five . . . in standing room."

Me: "I know. I remember."

Mother to me: "What's the first Broadway play you remember?"

"A *Tree Grows in Brooklyn.*'

"With Shirley Booth."

I recall the play very well. It was a lovely play, a lovely book that I've read and reread.

I ask my mother, "Where did you get this taste for culture?"

"I don't know. But when I was twelve, I and a group of four or five friends saved a nickel a week and went to a play downtown, as we called Manhattan."

My father drops the biggest surprise of all:

"Let me tell you where I got mine. You'll be shocked when I tell you. When I was fifteen or sixteen, I went to some place on the East Side. I went to a place where I did dancing, all sorts of modern dance."

Me: "Oh!"

"Yeah. In a gym. Boys and girls came and you stood and you did dancing."

"He was a good dancer and that was important."

"Yeah. I liked dancing. To me it was a lot of fun. Modern dancing as well as classical dancing . . . you know with two people . . ."

I've never known this. I don't think any of us children had.

My mother specifies, "He was also a ballroom dancer. There were kids who did sports and there were kids who did other things. And he liked dance and he liked plays."

Me to my father: "So you really have lived out your marriage vows—in sickness and in health, for richer or poorer."

"Oh, yeah. The only thing is that I get hysterical when she gets sick."

Me: "You've been together through . . ."

Mother finishes the sentence, "Thick and thin."

Me: "You kept your promise to each other."

Father: "In every way, in every way. She worked to do that also . . . increasing the family income. And she even had another baby after she was working."

Me: "Did you think there might be a better world, particularly after World War Two, after everybody had suffered so much? Didn't you think that people might have learned something?"

Mother: "We've lived a better life than I ever dreamed I would. When he made $2,000 a year we saved. One thing we don't talk about . . . that we had a good sex life."

Father: "Terrific!"

Mother: "Sex is an important part of the whole equation."

Father: ". . . sexual activity . . ."

Me: "Would you say it's the glue that glues things together?"

Mother: "We always had . . . have fun together too."

Father: "We took all of you. . . . We had fun. Didn't we?"

I nod. We did have tons of fun, roller skating, playing archery at Jones Beach in winter, all bundled up, with the wind howling. A million other things.

My father gets to his feet. "As a unit. I don't think I ever did anything alone."

Mother: "I don't think I did either, except professional things. I think we're lucky, we had and have the same major interests."

Mother and Father

"That's crucial."

Me: "So on all levels, you were, and are, good partners?"

Mother: "However, when I come back, I'm going to be an athlete."

I'm rendered speechless by this.

Father: "A what?"

"An athlete."

"And what about you when you're reincarnated?"

"I expect to spend a lovely time with her in heaven." He laughs.

Mother: "Oh, come on . . . the joy of our lives comes . . ."

"You don't understand how . . ."

". . . from our kids."

". . . crazy about the children she is."

Me: "Any regrets?"

Mother: "We should have been rich."

"When I finally made some money I gave her the money."

"The other thing that was great fun was that we enjoyed travel-ing. We first went to Europe in 'sixty-two. We were old by then, we were forty. We borrowed from my retirement."

"We had ten weeks."

"Eight weeks. We got to Italy and I schlepped him to the Blue Grotto because I remember the pictures in my geography book."

Me: "Ha, ha. You had to schlep him? He wouldn't go voluntarily?"

Father: "I didn't know what it was."

"He never went voluntarily."

"One minute! I took a picture. We went in a boat. We came to a place where there was sort of a mountain. There was something carved out and you had to bend back—lie down—to go under. I was astonished because anything you put in the water shone blue . . . luminescent."

"I can picture the geography book . . . the blue of it."

"We had a good time at every place we went."

"Every trip we took we found a beach. He wrote three textbooks and one thing on housing . . . and with a cat sitting on the table while he was working, typing."

"With two fingers. When I typed I could only use two fingers. But I was a fast typist. Also about forty articles."

Soon, my mother goes into her bedroom to take various medicines; my father and I go downstairs together. He to the cash machine at Citibank to check his balance, me to the E train back up to Chelsea.

"Dad, do you remember the words to 'Sam, You Made the Pants Too Long'?"

He sings:

"Sam, you made the pants too long,
You made the coat and vest
Fit the best,
But Sam, you made the pants too long."

His voice is still a resonant tenor.

"I don't remember the rest."

He lights a cigarette, looks very, very tired and battered by life. Once a man who sped down the street with the whole family running to catch up, accepting slowness is especially hard for him. He stops for breath.

"Sorry."

"It's nothing. Are your legs hurting?"

"No. It's my legs. They feel like they just won't carry me. Old age is a bitch. Your mother gets mad at me when I say it but it's true. Trivial things have become complex."

He reaches into his pocket and peels a twenty off the other bills.

"Don't take the subway today. Here. Take a taxi!"

He holds out the twenty to me. And, as we've lately done many times, we stand at the corner of Third Street and LaGuardia Place and argue about it.

Second Virginity

At some moment midway on a flight to Paris, there is a sudden rolling and a surging. I grip the armrests in fear; the woolly-haired (with the face of a crocodile) man next to me, who's been squeezing slices of lime into his drinks, reacts with merriment. We've been discussing favorite films from our youths—*Splendor in the Grass, Elmer Gantry, Last Picture Show, Annie Hall, The Sting.* He tells me that the very favorite film of his adolescence had once been Ingmar Bergman's *Wild Strawberries.*

"Did you ever see it? You might be a little too young."

"I saw it."

"Do you remember the part when the Swedish doctor looks at the clock?"

"I'm not sure."

"It's a large clock, a clock in the center of a town. He's walking through the town, looks at the clock and sees that the clock has no hands."

"Vaguely."

"I hadn't seen it in years. A few weeks ago I rented it and watched it with my daughter who's in high school."

"Did she like it?"

"She said she thought it was cool."

"Did you like it?"

"Not in the same way I liked it when I first saw it."

"Was it dated?"

"Not really. It was awfully slow. The doctor's daughter is very stiff. And the doctor . . ." he laughs. "I remembered him as an old man. But, seeing it now, I saw that he wasn't old at all. He was about the same age as me. In many ways it seemed like a movie I'd never seen. It was as if I was seeing it for the very first time."

Eventually the turbulence calms and I doze. Though most of the shades are drawn in order for people to sleep or watch the film being shown, ours hasn't been completely pulled, and when I wake I can see the milky light in the sky that means it's morning in Paris. I open the book of poems by Philip Larkin that I've brought to read. Just after they announce the beginning of our descent into Charles de Gaulle Airport, I read and mark a poem called "Faith Healing."

> *In everyone there sleeps*
> *A sense of life lived according to love.*
> *To some it means the difference they could make*
> *By loving others, but across most it sweeps*
> *As all they might have done had they been loved.*

I plan to begin my next interview by discussing Larkin's poem, but, as it turns out, I don't.

"The heart doesn't always obey linear time"

In Paris I meet with Louis Barr, who is a Scottish novelist and translator. He's tall and thin, has a stiff spine, close-cropped, dark, thinning hair, a thick, full mustache and a Roman nose. He's forty-six. He's been based in Paris for twenty years. Because his newest book has just been delivered to his publisher, he has some free time. He's worn out, his throat hurts, his stomach aches, yet he receives me with an appealing smile. Two years before, he'd split up with a woman he'd known for ten years, and had lived with for eight.

"I've been trying to allow that to pass with as little nastiness as possible, and then starting something new, with the difficulty that the heart doesn't always obey linear time . . . beginning again and also repeating. You go forward and backward, you're not quite sure where you are, mourning and excitement and overlap."

He is now involved with a Bulgarian woman whom he first met at one of his book signings and whom—after he had broken off his relationship—he had gotten to know by e-mail.

"Slowly," he tells me.

After many months of buildup, a love affair began.

"I've been experiencing an exciting resurgence of sexual activity and most exciting of all is that I'm enjoying kissing for the first time in my life!"

Louis is wonderful to listen to. He speaks with a slight Scottish accent, gesturing often with his long hands. My hopes for a frank no-holds-barred talk about this sexual resurgence during our conversation at his Paris apartment are dashed when he begins to salt his talk with references to writers and texts. By the end of our conversation we've consumed a bathtub of good espresso, and his coffee table is littered with books lying facedown, open to various passages. Nonetheless, in its way, I've found the interview extremely sexy.

Milan Kundera's *Immortality* is the first book he pulls from the wall-to-wall bookshelf.

"Kundera talks about the various erotic stages of life as a 'dial of life' . . . a clock."

He thumbs through the chapters, picks out a passage and reads with a deep, courtly voice:

> *"Your life will always be built from the same materials, the same bricks, the same problems, and what will seem to you at first a new life will soon turn out to be just a variation of your old existence."*

Will it? I wonder. I sit at one end of a soft, apple green couch. He's at the other end.

> *"When we're young, we can't imagine that our lives will be variations on the same theme and that at some point, someone will use the phrase 'when you were young.' But by the second act we realize that youth is something that has passed. And then . . ."*

He pauses, gives me a look that says, Listen carefully, and reads:

> *". . . he told himself that there would be no harm in taking a brief pause in his relations with women. Until next time, as they say. But this pause kept getting longer week by week, month by month. One day he realized that there would be no 'next time.'"*

He drops the book and we lock eyes. His face has gotten very pale.

. . .

After I've spoken with Louis, I speak with Margarita Lalova, Louis's girlfriend. She and I sit on the same green couch. She hasn't an ounce of fat on her small frame. Her lustrous, dark hair is shoulder length. When she smiles, her eyes sparkle playfully. She came to Paris a number of years ago after receiving a scholarship to study. Now she's working for a multinational corporation. She explains that, when she was young, she felt bigger than the small town in Bulgaria where she grew up.

"Since I was a child, I have never been attracted by the quiet, or by the conventional. I wanted to travel and see the world and be amazed. I wanted to meet someone whose mind and body would be surprising to me every day. I had been dreaming of someone who would dazzle me."

Leaving her home and post-Communist Bulgaria, with its conservative traditions and devastated economy, was the hardest thing she'd ever done. Not only because her parents didn't want to see her leave, but because there were things like visa, money, temptations.

"When you grow up under communism, you are told that 'the other side' is full of dangerous people. I said good-bye to my family at the airport, and it was a strange moment when the customs office separated them from me with a glass wall. I could see them through a glass. They were crying. During the flight there was a spectacular storm—the plane was shaking. It was quite shocking. But then Paris emerged like an enormous piece of jewelry, diamonds spilled everywhere."

One evening, she went to a reading Louis was giving.

"The first thing I noticed about him was the beautiful gestures, thin fingers, like an insect . . . orchestrating," she laughs. "Later, when I asked if he noticed me, he said, 'Yes, you were like a little mouse in the corner.'"

After the reading, she presented Louis with a bouquet of white daisies she had run out to buy minutes earlier. When she approached Louis he was sitting on the candle-lined café stairway, signing books piled on his knees.

"This was the first moment I started to desire him."

"Erotically?"

"He was wearing red trousers and a black shirt. I remember thinking, He should just flip it around, black trousers, red shirt. I thought he would have been irresistible then."

"Erotically?"

"Yes. But not only. I began to desire him in every way. He signed my book and I thought, This is really scary, really dangerous. This man is too popular, especially with the ladies. I noticed a sexy girl with large breasts dressed like Britney Spears, porno chic clothes, waiting in line with a book to be signed, his eyes taking her in."

Margarita left the reading quite early, and they lost contact until she thought to e-mail Louis some Bulgarian poems. He replied the same day, complimenting her Balkan ancestors on their passion, on their romantic souls. Pretty soon afterward, they were exchanging e-mails every day.

Back to Louis:

"In act two, when you've gone beyond youth, you tend to be much more finicky and demanding about the person you're with. So actually it's less likely you'll meet a person who appeals to all of you. I think that's one of the big challenges. You might find someone who appeals to a bit of you, some aspect of you, but to all of your body, never mind all of your mind, this becomes much less probable. You wonder if you'd not be better off alone. As one ages one becomes more selfish and greedy—read Muriel Spark on old people—and in the same time one is more finicky, set in one's ways, tempted by solitude."

He pauses to sip his espresso.

"On top of that, what my male contemporaries also worry about is a type of lessening . . . an altering of libidinous urges and the loss of confidence that goes with that. You're looking at a point where you'll no longer be as functional or as successful as you have been. I'm not talking only about genital libido. Women can always spread their legs, get wet, or so I would imagine. For a man, however, no matter how intimate and confident the sex, there's always a performance. And what if one doesn't get quite as many erections, and if they don't sustain themselves quite so well?"

He sighs and stands up, bringing his arm around toward his lower back. He starts to pace with the palm of his hand kneading his lower spine.

"Are you all right?"

"My back's aching, but never mind."

He sits back down.

"This is when the second act narrative starts. 'Oh, I don't mind,' says the other, if one is lucky. 'You know, I love you just the same.' They're all compensatory, they're all sad. That's what we're told we have to look forward to in one's future. I've been fortunate in that area so far, though not necessarily in other areas. I'm not being boastful. There's something onerous about being a man. Not by chance, I'm reading a book about Pompeii, where people wore phalluses around their necks. Italian men are constantly touching themselves. When you see a priest, when you see a nun, when they see chastity, they touch their balls to ensure these are still functioning."

He fiddles with his mustache.

"I think the challenge of the second act may be to find a narra-tive of sexual engagement that isn't genitally driven, and yet isn't sad and passionless either; isn't—'Yes, you're okay *but* . . .'—to find some other narrative that isn't just a story of decline. Where are the areas in which I have failed to move in my sexuality? What have I failed to explore? We talked about the mouth—I've always had trouble with my mouth."

To find a way out of such an impasse, he admitted that he needed a good deal of inner probing and a good deal of luck in the person he encountered.

"I'm someone who's fascinated by mouths. My world is a word world. I'm fascinated by Beckett, and no one has a more acute sense of the possibility of the mouth as an orifice, right down to the play *Not I*, which is just a mouth. Utterance. The writers I like tend to appeal to the ear—they're writers who are good to read out loud. Ear and mouth. Kundera talks about the 'period of obscenity,' when suddenly you find a thrill in using obscene language and you think that you invented it. If you hear another person using it you think, Oh, they must have heard me using it. I think it's almost im-possible to be obscene in a foreign language. You can use the ob-scene words but you don't feel the impact. They make you laugh."

Louis walks into the kitchen. He returns with a plate on which a few crackers have been smeared with smelly cheese. He eats one. I eat one.

"Where were we?"

"Obscenity."

"Oh, yes. Alas, I'm not someone who found the language of obscenity—of love and sex—particularly easy. I'm someone who con-trols his words too closely. And for reasons which I still don't fully un-derstand, I've experienced a mouth problem, which has manifested itself not only in words but also in kissing. There's something about the moment in which the visual yields to the sensual which I find . . . I go into an anxious mode. When someone comes too close, especially with their own eyes . . . where I simply can't focus."

"What if it's dark?"

"Dark doesn't help. The mouth is used for many things, for giving out words, for ingesting food, for suckling, spitting, breathing in and out. Again Beckett is the best person on that—*two holes and me in the middle*. Then, there's something alarming about putting things in the mouth and swallowing them. Once in the mouth they cease to exist as objects. I've had a problem with eating ever since childhood. My ideal meal would be a beautiful, large white plate with some intricate Japanese perfection on it, to be admired and then to be taken away. Or, somehow to digest the meal without demolishing it. The mouth for pleasure, the mouth which absorbs, the mouth which destroys."

"In the past, would you kiss someone or would you avoid it?"

"It was a passage I'd try to get through as quickly as possible. The kiss was the door, while other pleasures lay beyond the door. It just felt unnatural to me. It felt like, Oh God, do we really have to?"

"Did anyone ever say you're a lousy kisser?"

"Yeah."

"Or don't you like kissing? Or don't I taste good?"

"All of the above. Don't you like it? Why don't you like it? You've got a problem with your mouth."

"All this was before Margarita?"

"Yes. Before."

Back to Margarita:

With feeling, she explains that looking forward to his e-mails quickly became an exciting expectation.

"I needed to read his lines in the evening, before I went to bed."

Sometimes she read an e-mail five or six times a day to re-experience the beautiful string of words.

"He took me places with words I never imagined existed. I keep all his letters, which unroll like a sensual love story, on my computer."

The summer after they met, she went back to Bulgaria for a traditional holiday on the Black Sea coast, where for once the weather was terrible.

"I sat in a terrace café above the sea wondering what to do with the rain and my new strong feelings for Louis. In a way, it was crazy. I thought that our families would object, and that our language and cultures would clash, but I also knew that I would always regret not having satisfied my curiosity, discovering what would happen later. So I wrote Louis a real letter, an invitation to weave our feelings into reality, and I sent it, hoping it would make it through the storm all the way to Scotland where he was visiting his mother."

I ask her to tell me a bit about her earlier amorous experiences.

"The first time I fell in love, I was thirteen. He was my brother's best friend and also my childhood Indiana Jones. He was beautiful physically, like a god, long blond hair, tall, slim but fit. I looked up to him more for all the books he had read and the places he was interested in. On his fifteenth birthday he invited me to his party and we sat in the same chair. Two people in one chair. He was very silent, had a serious face as if something dramatic had happened, as if we were going to die. I could feel he wanted to tell me he loved me and I was so scared. And then he did and I kept quiet. The confession was so intense that it terrified me into silence. I couldn't say anything back. I haven't been able to since then. Louis was the first man to whom I said 'I love you' out loud."

Margarita and the boy were a couple until she was sixteen. On her sixteenth birthday, they made love. But in high school she moved into a larger circle, and her boyfriend stayed in that smaller circle and fell behind. She broke up with him.

Back to Louis and his thoughts about kissing:

"You think—Kissing!—that's overrated. Given that the range of sexual activities is large, everyone has something they don't like doing. I tried to compensate. Perhaps my fear was of swallowing the person whole, which really is an infant's fear . . . goes back a long way, beyond even the early death of my father—a very complex desire and repression—affixing itself to my mouth. Trying to undo such an inhibition: I think this is the only hope for the second act. To find someone to loosen up these inhibitions."

He got to know Margarita slowly.

"I had to relive adolescence. There was a long buildup, until I felt able to give my lips for the first time."

"Maybe she took them?"

He ponders my comment, then says, "It's harder and harder to be surprised in the second act, and yet you've got to be surprised. This change surprised me."

"Have you always had a mustache, by the way?"

"Not in childhood."

"Ha, ha. Could that somehow impact kissing?"

"Yeah. Not by chance that Margarita said from early on, 'Oh! I like your mustache.'"

"Did women in the past not like your mustache?"

"Not particularly."

Margarita walks into the room with a bowl of juicy-looking plums from Spain and puts them down on the coffee table. Louis immediately reaches for the largest plum and takes a bite. She kisses him on the top of his head and tiptoes out of the room.

"As against that freedom, remember what I was saying earlier, about becoming pernickety as one grows older, this links in with the lure of solitude. I've learned to enjoy living alone, and that includes enjoying my own idiosyncrasies and obsessions."

He cradles the pit of the plum in his palm, then takes it into the kitchen to the disposal.

"I see many of my contemporaries, male especially, around their mid-forties, trying to convince themselves that they like solitude but really just becoming attached to their habits and finding it harder to connect with people. Their hearts, bruised too often, having more and more trouble to open again. I see the pleasure I've learned to experience in solitude as potentially very dangerous. I don't want to start polishing my car and mowing my lawn. I don't own a car or a lawn!"

The irritating noise of human voices drifts up from the pedestrian street—the Rue Montorgueil.

Back to Margarita:

She was happy that she'd had the courage to send the letter from Bulgaria because it interrupted the slow routine of their getting to know each other. After they'd both returned to Paris they went out for their first dinner.

"I could see he was all lit up when he saw me. Sparkling in his eyes. I said, 'Wow.' After, I didn't want to go home. We just sat on the station platform and the train passed and another train passed."

Shortly afterward, Louis left for Bellagio in Italy on a fellowship.

"One day he called me from Italy and the call lasted for more than an hour. From then on, we started speaking on the phone almost every day, and this moved us a step closer to each other as our voices caressed each other through the phone. The fact that we had bodies became more real than through mail. One day Louis asked me, 'Would you like to come to Italy . . . to a little place near Bellagio?' I said, 'I don't know.' Suddenly I hesitated, maybe because I realized the depth of my feelings and the need to be with this man. He called and said, 'There's a train.' I decided that if I didn't see him, something would have been lost."

The next day Margarita took the overnight train, had to change trains in Milan at dawn.

"The train was packed. It was stuffy. The longest moment in my life was when we were entering the station. I saw him the moment I came down from the train. He was absolutely beautiful in his sandals; his cheeks and toes very tanned. Superb. Light linen pants. He didn't look worried or sad. He came to me, smiling. I said, 'Don't touch me.' I was hot and smelly. He said, 'Hmmm, how little you know me.' "

Back to Louis:

"Italy was an incredible time—learning to kiss, learning Italian."

He sidetracks. "Scottish people have thin lips. They often don't seem to have lips. Scottish people hardly open their mouths when they're talking, maybe because it's so damn cold. When I was studying Italian, my teacher said, 'You're never going to speak Italian if you don't open your mouth.' "

He demonstrates with his lips closed.

"*Allora* . . ."

Then he opens his mouth wide.

"*Allora!* For me it was fascinating and terrifying: massive expansion and contraction of the mouth. When I was learning basic Italian, and would go to Italy and say three or four words, the Italians would say, '*Que brava!* You speak Italian so well, where did you learn?' And suddenly I'd find the words flowing out. Words I didn't know I knew. I'd barely have time to think. Speaking a new language, speaking new words of love, and kissing too for that matter—they're all ways of using my mouth in a new way. So perhaps my route to happiness in the second act will be through the surprises that mouths have to offer."

He pauses, picks up another plum and puts it down uneaten.

"All of Proust's novel is there in the first page. It's a particular unlinear type of narrative, unlike George Eliot's, which is certainly not all there in the first page. I think life corresponds to the Proustian experience—that we keep on expanding that ripple. Our sexual selves, our love selves, are like that too. In act two we need a way to interfere with that ripply pattern, which is a repeat pattern. If we're very lucky, we may find someone who says, 'Oh, I like that, I like that inhibition. That excites me. You do that so well.'"

Back to Margarita:

"In the bus we both looked so serious. We didn't speak. I was tired, half falling asleep. When we arrived, we stopped in a café for a coffee, a juice. We were silent and excited. Then we carried my many bags to a little hotel."

Louis suggested a little rest. Afterward they'd go out to dinner. Margarita told him she wanted to wash off, wash her hair.

"I'd given him a large honey soap some months before because I liked its sweet heavy perfume and its shape, which was that of a bee. When he came into the bathroom, I was surprised to see this soap in his hand; he had brought it to Italy with him. 'I'm going to wash you,' he said. 'All right, come up,' I told him, feeling like an excited child."

"You've told me that you never said 'I love you' before. How was this different from your other relationships?"

"My heart opened. I felt ready to say it. It was complete, very real, the feeling of being in love."

Back to Louis:

"Writers are more than ever our friends in the second act. Friends, more than teachers. There's no greater dissector of the human soul than Proust. Jealousy, for example. Not that reading Proust will stop you from being jealous, but you can't really have a simple jealous knee jerk if you've read his work in detail. If you're jealous, really in the throes of it, you'll have Swann there, the jealous companion. You can speak to him and think about yourself through him."

"What about Beckett?"

"With Beckett there's no first act, not even in his early work. He never writes his *Portrait of the Artist* about the person who's making it who says at the end, 'This is my destiny, this is my future.' Beckett's characters are forever being crippled, watching life erode, in decline. And this is why they're the ideal second-act companions. What's so fascinating is that Beckett's is never a story of ending. The second act is about the fact that you can't imagine your ending, even though you know it's approaching. Second act is a loss of immortality with the big catch that you don't know what this means, unless you're religious, a believer with faith. If you're religious, you know what it is to die. The rest of us don't. One is constantly imagining something that's unimaginable."

He rubs the back of his neck.

"Proust said that we picture growing old as a shocking event. But it isn't that, it's the day you wake up and you can't quite tie your shoelaces, or it's painful to pee. It's incremental, hard to capture. We imagine an apocalypse. It's not. There's no way out of that. It's rather a decline. It's a complete pisser not to know what death means, and yet to know it's going to happen. That certainty of uncertainty. If there's to be love in the second act, somehow it has to grow out of that certainty of uncertainty, out of the embrace of what is not tolerable. '*Born astride a grave with a difficult birth,*' Vladimir says in *Waiting for Godot,* something like—'*It's out in a candle, your life.*'"

"Go on."

"For men there may be a special twist to growing older, as even in our prime we're not so great! Men can't be as promiscuous as women. This, I think, creates an anxiety in men that used to manifest itself in demands of virginity and fidelity. When Tiresias, who lived as a man and as a woman, was summoned to Mount Olympus and asked who had greater pleasure in the sexual act, men or women, he said women have nine times more pleasure than men. At this point he was blinded. But then Zeus gave him the compensatory power of second sight. I don't know if women have nine times more, but I do suspect that my personal sense of a second act is reinforced by a historically renewed consciousness of the limitation of men, a general understanding of the decline of our usefulness. With sperm banks, men are more than ever redundant. How will we men compensate for our redundancy? We're not doing well. We're gauche. We're violent. We have to find some new route to necessity."

There's another burst of intrusive noise outside. We walk over to the window together and see again that the street is full of people walking and talking.

"I'm fortunate in that I'm experiencing the animal self, the instinctual, the spontaneous, the explosion between two people. But when that becomes problematic, which it inevitably will later in the second act, how will I find a way of being that's not just coziness and companionship and niceness? Maybe that's where what has happened to my mouth becomes important, an indication . . . a passage . . . a hope for the future when I'm not simply looking at death, saying, 'It's better going together than going alone.'"

"You're a good talker. Do women fall in love with you because of it?"

"Not consciously. When I'm talking about the books I love, people can fall in love with me, but of course it's not really with me. They're falling in love with the fact that I love this book. That's transference. They think they're falling in love with me but they're falling in love with Proust, the feeling that I have for Proust. It can only lead to frustration. It's like falling in love with your therapist, a boring old fart in a chair."

"And happiness? In the second act?"

He leaves me hanging when the doorbell rings. Though his exchange with the caller only lasts a minute, it feels like more. He returns carrying a package the size of a book.

"There may indeed be a new sort of happiness in the second act. I really believe so. For in the second act, you're aware that there *is* a second act. The horizon of mortality is there. That's the challenge and the promise of the second act, not just my troubled mouth, not just my sore knee. No, rather, can I use my body in a new way that gives it . . . gives me and the other . . . not just compensation, but a new fullness? In the second act you know that nothing lasts, yet you know for this very reason that love *may* last. Plato said it a long time ago, love is giving what you do not have. In the second act, we are much more aware of what we do not have. Making the most of what one does not have, giving the most of what one does not have. That's what I'm hoping for in the second act."

Back to Margarita:

"Back in Paris, he invited me out for dinner one evening. He took me for an amazing meal. He seemed very nervous. After dinner I said, 'What happened?' He said, 'Let's walk around.' I said, 'Tell me.' He wouldn't. We went to the Palais Royal gardens, sat on a bench. He told me he loved me. He kissed me. It was a slow kiss at first, our lips barely touching, his mustache tickling my cheeks, then deeper. I drank from his tongue and heart. He said, 'I want it to be forever.' He'd opened his heart for me and I loved him back."

Her eyes shine.

"We walked to a posh part of town to Rue Montorgueil. He said, 'I really want you to meet someone.' 'Who, who? Not Samuel Beckett?' He led me up some steps, opened the door here and said, 'I want you to meet the new me. I'm living here now.'"

"Do you feel a sense of destiny? Fate? That you belong together?"

"I'm very glad we found each other. I'm very glad it happened."

"Do you think this is as good as it gets? Like you hit a jackpot?"

"I really love him. I want to take it as it comes. It's not always easy. I'm in love and that's enough for now."

A few weeks later, I receive a letter from Margarita from Tahiti.

You won't believe how great he looks now, tanned and strong. We keep swimming as much as possible in the sea. It is such a happy, sexy time, that the spirits of the place have been forever soaked with kisses, with body fluids.

Yesterday, after being in bed for some hours in the afternoon, Louis called for me to join him in the courtyard of our rented house. I did and as I stepped out of the house he told me to take my dress off and lie on the tiles and close my eyes. The ground was so hot, my bottom was burning and I was trying to guess what he was dreaming up. Suddenly, all over me, he poured freezing water from the well. The feeling was so shocking but also terribly exciting and he went on pouring water over me until I begged him to come closer and kiss me again. . . .

"I didn't want to end up with my cats"

I've taken the high-speed train from Gare du Nord in Paris to Brussels Midi on a gray Saturday morning to interview an American woman living in Brussels who, after being fixed up by a friend, began an affair with another woman. The American's name is Odile Duflot. She's originally from Minnesota.

On the train, while nibbling on the little box lunch given out in first class, I shuffle through my file folder—the second one, number two—to catch up with bits and pieces I hadn't yet read. One, an article called "Hello, Old Love" by Sarah Mahoney, discusses the recent upsurge in what the writer calls "rekindling." This is described as the trend in which, thanks to the Internet, people have been looking for, and reconnecting with, their "old flames." The article posits that the occurrence of a "significant birthday," such as fifty or sixty, is usually what kick-starts the desire to reconnect with our youthful selves. Mahoney also discusses other potential rekindling triggers, including divorce, the empty-nest syndrome, the death of parents and friends, and physical changes.

Next I find the following passage from a Xerox copy of an essay by Sy Safransky called "Some Enchanted Evening":

What have I craved more than a woman's arms? To be up half the night, talking, laughing, making love—have I ever been closer to heaven? The bed becomes your church: you pass the collection plate back and forth until you've given too much, then your poverty becomes your gift: your tears, her tears—I mean, when it's right, who can tell laughing from crying? And though, in days or months or years to come, you'll swear you were fooling yourself, you weren't, it really happened: in the midst of all that fluttering, between the spilled wine and the giggling and the breathless kiss, your hearts billowed out like great white sails, and above you for a moment hovered the dove.

I decide to take a break from love, zip up my little backpack and watch the slumbering fields of northern France as the train speeds past them. Pure Corot.

I meet Odile at her apartment in Brussels. There are three small black kittens curled around each other in a cardboard box on the floor. When we're seated in a kind of breakfast nook, I read her the Safransky quote.

Her comment: "Six weeks ago I'd have yawned. Now that I've come alive again it brings tears to my eye."

I notice that her ears have turned red. She pours herself a glass of red table wine. When I decline a glassful, she brings me a lemon drink. On the table is a bowl of sunflower seeds. Irresistible. I take one. Another. A handful.

"What is your work exactly?" I ask as I crack a seed with my front teeth.

"I work for an international aid organization."

The kittens start squealing. The gray mother cat strides out from somewhere and climbs into the box. The kittens crowd under her for milk.

"I love my work. For many years I'd been traveling so much that my romantic life was put onto a back burner. Then, a few months ago, I was given a big promotion. It meant less travel, so I began to spend more time here in Brussels, where our organization is based."

"What made you want to move your romantic life from the back to the front burner?"

"Horniness. Loneliness. Seeing the writing on the wall when I hit fifty that sixty wasn't too far off. I didn't want to end up alone or alone with my cats, or with birds, or dogs, or an aquarium or all of the above."

"Weren't you horny and lonely before then?"

"Actually not. During my years of travel I was so busy that, quite frankly, I wasn't ever horny. Wait . . . that's not exactly true. This may sound odd, but for me hard work is a kind of aphrodisiac. There's no way to explain why, it simply has a component of excitement that is akin to sex, substitutes for sex. Once I stopped traveling, some of that work obsession dissipated, and a craving for an actual someone in my bed replaced it. The craving got so strong, I could practically taste it. But how to get into circulation after so many years out of circulation? That was the question. I was scared to death. It wasn't just that. Being bisexual, I've always been mired in conflict about exactly what it is that I really want. And—

at this juncture in my life—I still have no idea. Did I want women? Men? Did I want old? Young? All I knew was that I began to crave sex and wanted more than anything to experience the feeling of being in love. Once it didn't seem such a bad idea to grow old with my cats but suddenly it didn't seem to be enough. Around that time I began to correspond with Irena."

"And?"

"When a friend gave me Irena's address, despite my general feeling of ambivalence, it was the perfect way to at least get my feet wet, by putting pen to paper."

"Didn't it bother you that Irena lived in another country, another city?"

The mother cat steps over the lip of the cardboard, jumps out and leaves the room.

"No. Amsterdam's not much more than two hours on a fast train from here. If I were living in Minneapolis, it would be like dating someone in Duluth. Plus, I'm not exactly out of the closet at work . . . not that they'd care if they knew. It's me—I'm the secretive one."

"What was the progression of the letter writing that led to a meeting?"

"First we tested the water. We exchanged a few letters. Then we exchanged photos. Then more letters. Then we set up a meeting."

The plan was Odile would take an afternoon train to Amsterdam and Irena would pick her up at Central Station. From there, they would go together by local train to a little place they'd rented near the North Sea and spend some time together.

"You see we agreed by letter that we would not give each other enough of a chance to get acquainted if we just met for a meal or a drink."

"And?"

She laughs.

"At the meeting point, I saw the woman I recognized from the photos we'd exchanged, holding a huge bouquet of red roses and another of yellow roses and smiling. She was dressed like a woman out of a Matisse, in a long colored skirt, and had a Degas body. Shamefully, I hadn't thought to bring flowers. You see I really *am* out of practice."

They caught a local train for the coast about ten minutes later, made lame conversation during the train ride while looking each other over. Odile describes Irena as having choppy brown hair, green eyes and Slavic cheekbones. Although Irena spoke good Dutch, Czech, Russian and German, Odile quickly realized her written English was much better than her spoken English. In counterpoint to Irene's colorful attire, Odile wore tailored slacks and jacket, both black, with a blue knitted sweater underneath and a heavy silver bracelet on her wrist. Odile is myopic; although she has white hair, she has a youthful face and a nose that could be likened to Virgina Woolf's. Odile also has what we in America call a "full" body.

"As we traveled, a sad sun tried to break through the mist, but failed. The weather was unusually warm for Holland. It was also misty."

If nothing came of their sojourn, they hoped to enjoy a nice little holiday together.

"Of course there had to be two bedrooms. When we got off the train, it was dark. She took my suitcase and I let her. She led us along a road. It seemed like she'd been there before. I could hear the gurgling of the sea. A storm was developing and wind began to gust. Her Matisse skirt whipped up. It was a patchwork of plaids and prints, geometric swatches of material sewn together. 'I don't wear underpants!' she volunteered, not stopping the wind from having its way with her skirt. The cottage had two rooms, beds in each. She found vases for the roses. From her rucksack, Irena took a bottle of a special vodka made in the Czech Republic. A sip of the fiery liquid was all I could take right then. We sat on the little porch, in sweaters, and watched the eerie shadow of the moon, in and out of the mist. Then we went to bed, she in hers, me in mine. I knew I wanted to sleep with her from the moment she'd mentioned that she didn't wear underpants, and all night I felt an ache . . . like a nagging splinter under a nail."

Since English didn't come easy to Irena, they hardly spoke. Although Odile knew French, Irena didn't.

"On the second night the weather changed. The wind died and the sky cleared, showing stars. After supper we took another walk. She told me that she had walked across Nepal with a lover, had walked in Finland, Czechia—as she called her homeland— Germany, across Mongolia, Kyrgyzstan because of knowing Russian. And more. I was very impressed."

On Odile's side table there's a wooden breadboard on which is bread and butter and liver paste.

"The next morning was fresh. But the temperature rose again. By afternoon it was unpleasant. When I lay down for an afternoon rest after the walk, I told Irena she could lie down with me, that it was cooler in my room. I picked up my book. She lay down beside me. I could see by her cherry-red face that she was suffering from the heat. She was soaking wet and her clothes were drenched as well. She went and got a towel, wiped herself down. Then she turned on her side, wrapped herself up in the bedsheet she'd taken from her bed and fell asleep. She slept for about an hour, then woke and smiled at me. I went to get her a glass of cool water and when I returned I saw that she was drenched again."

While I spread the liver paste onto bread, Odile describes how Irena prepared a meal of boiled potatoes, butter and garlic, also serving some kind of cold vinegary Czech cucumber and herb salad.

"The meal was the farthest thing from nouvelle cuisine I'd tasted in years. It was delicious. *She and She* is the title of a painting that

She and She

Irena had done. She'd made a photo of it as a gift, and gave it to me after dinner that night. It's two Matisse-like women whose hips have spread."

Odile points up at the framed photo of the painting on her wall.

"After finishing the potatoes, she told me to shower and dress up; she had a surprise planned for me. I showered, shaved my legs, washed my hair, then realized I had nothing dressy to wear. I put on a black silk slip and was going to put on a linen skirt but Irena peeked into my room and, seeing me, said, 'That's good enough.' So I stopped there, feeling kind of brash. Evening was coming. She lit incense and also a red pyramid-shaped candle, and broke the seal of a pack of New Age–style cards she'd brought with her. I felt quite apprehensive. She shuffled the cards, took one for herself, told me to pick a card. Her card read Healing. Mine read Surrender."

We smile.

"'Now you must sing along,' she ordered, and handed me a sheet of writing paper decorated with two swooning, Disney-esque sleeping beauties, a heart between them, with words on it. She slipped a cassette into a cassette player. It was a folk song about two women who pick each other up in a market in Germany at the vegetable counter, then follow each other around, buying cheese, lamb chops, and chocolate. I'm not sure if she took me by the hand and led me, or if I followed her inside. She kissed me until my toes began to curl. Forgive me if I omit the details."

Irena took Odile on several beautiful walks in the next three days.

"The first walk was to Zandvoort aan Zee, a marked trail through sandy fields. There were birds in profusion in wooded areas, small lakes, gladiolus and a stark cross on a dune commemorating a martyred woman in the Resistance. She had been shot by the Germans at the very spot on which the cross stood. We looked across high grassy dunes beside the North Sea while we sat and ate our sandwiches. Then we made love. We passed fields, duck ponds in which scudding clouds were reflected as well as a white lighthouse. We stopped to eat more sandwiches, saw two lone rabbits fucking which they interrupted when they saw us watching them."

Their final walk was even longer.

"The weather got gray and drizzly again. The following day we began our walk along the shoreline, past children wearing jackets digging in the sand. Soon the beach was deserted except for sandpipers and gulls. We walked for about an hour. The skies lightened, the drizzle stopped. Irena told me about two dreams she'd had the night before: First dream: 'I dreamed I found a baby on the airplane to Brussels. It was a nice baby. I took it.' Second one: 'I dreamed your father wasn't right. He sent you money and we had to go to him in Minnesota. But we had to walk there.'"

"Interesting."

"We sat together in the sand, kissed a bit, then ate our sandwiches. Soon we continued on toward an area of shoreline bordered by high dunes, which, as we got close, revealed nude men standing in the dunes cruising each other. We walked a little further, the sea was suddenly sparkling in sunlight. I saw a very, very old man and woman walking toward us naked. I'd never seen the genitals of an old man or an old woman before. We walked to the village of Camperduin. My ankles hurt. It had been a mistake to take off my shoes and walk barefoot in the sand."

On the fifth day there, they took the train back. Odile had to make a short business trip to Berlin, so she got off at Schiphol Airport. Things had gone so well they'd decided she'd fly back to Amsterdam when her work was completed. In Berlin, Odile checked her e-mail for the first time in a week. She e-mailed her friend Gerry in Philadelphia:

It's been perfect. She has green eyes, the body of a Degas and hardly speaks any English.

When Odile got back from her business meeting Gerry had replied:

Green eyes and fourth-grade English. How unimprovable.

We laugh together. Then I turn off my recorder. She pushes our pile of sunflower seeds aside and serves us both a slice of quiche and a small salad. When we've finished eating, she asks if I've had enough.

"Of food or of the story of your tryst?"

"The story."

"Is there more?"

"Yes. Again, we met at the meeting point in Central Station. It was my birthday, you see. Again she carried my luggage. She took me along a canal to her little room, or, as she calls it, 'mine little hut.' It has huge double windows, probably fifteen feet high, that look out on the back gardens. Her walls are chockablock with her large, bright paintings, including the original of *She and She*— perhaps four-by-four. There is a loft that contains a large mattress and a pile of folded eiderdown at the foot. One reaches the bed by a steep wooden ladder. Every surface of the room is filled with various kinds of clutter, racks holding dozens of her Matisse skirts and other clothing, which she told me she finds at the second-hand market for one euro each. Fancy carafes and snifters for brandy and other alcohols clutter a countertop."

The mother cat strides into the room and rubs against Odile's legs.

"On the table was fresh bread, cheese, butter and liverwurst that I like. We sat down and, just as we began to eat, she turned red and broke out into a sweat. 'I had one hundred of these on the day I got back from the North Sea. Menopause. Hot flashes,' she told me, and showed me a booklet titled 'Change of Life: Holistic Treatments' written in English. 'My book on Chinese medicine said to drink potato drink and beet drink. In the afternoon. Now.' She proceeded to peel two potatoes and stuff them into a blender, and drink down the results."

The mother cat hops back into the cardboard carton and begins to lick the kittens. They don't seem to like being licked.

"When we'd eaten, she ordered me, 'Take off your clothes. Everything. I'll wash you.' I stripped off my clothes and together we stood under her shower. She scrubbed me with lavender-smelling

soap, my hair with another aromatic, herbal shampoo. She gathered up my dirty clothes, underwear, shoes and all. Then she
wrapped me in a bath towel and I followed her up into the loft bed.
She'd brought various massage creams and oils. 'Now relax,' she ordered, and went to work on me with two strong hands while I shut
my eyes. She didn't tire, massaged me for hours. Finally, when I'd
been rubbed within an inch of my life, her hands changed tack, her
mouth covered mine with kisses. The next day was my birthday.
After that, I had to get to a meeting in Brussels, and she was leaving for a monthlong walk across the Crimea with a friend. Her
huge rucksack was packed and was leaning against the wall. We
spent all afternoon in bed, making love. When Irena got up and
stood on the wooden stairway naked, she ordered, 'Stay!'—which
I was glad to do. Satiated, I fell into a deep sleep, and was visited by
the delightful smell of garlic. I woke when she called me, and I saw
a pile of my freshly laundered clothes beside me. Holding onto the
wall, I descended the ladder. She ordered, 'Sit!' "

The mother cat jumps when Odile exclaims.

"Spread across the table were wrapped packages. There were
amber crystal wineglasses, a bottle of Belgian blackberry wine,
candles, cloth napkins, bowls of salad, our favorite boiled potatoes
with fresh dill, garlic and more. Then she carried over a heavy
black frying pan. Inside, still sizzling, were two silver gray and black
trout, side by side, drizzled with various spices and butters. 'We
make it this way in Czechia.' Finally, when all was consumed, all
packages opened, presents spread among the dirty plates and
glasses, she revealed a large cake that was shaped like a heart. It
was slathered with swirling pink and green icing reading 'Happy
Birthday Odile!' "

"Nice."

"All the while, outside the window, the rain poured down in deluge. 'You promised you'd massage *my* bips,' she reminded me. Bips was the word she used for her buttocks. She drank down a glass of puréed potato for hot flash, leaving a white mustache on her lip. That night, our last. She drank a lot of wine. In bed I began massaging her feet, toes, arch, Achilles' heel and ankles. I took all the time in the world. All the while she was as silent as a little lamb. I loved the feel of her earthbound body."

Odile stops speaking and begins to stack the plates.

"Is that it?"

"Yes. Except I didn't know it at the time, but she'd been asleep the whole while I'd been massaging her."

We crack up.

"That was three months ago. Next week she'll be back in her 'little hut' in Amsterdam. I don't know if I'll hear from her. If I don't, I don't know what I'll do with my yearning."

One kitten squeals. The mother cat's teeth are sunk into its neck.

"Would you like to take a cat back to New York with you? They're ordinary *chat de gouttière* . . . but they'll love you to death."

"I wouldn't mind," I answer, but—after teetering on the brink of saying yes—I decline the offer. I wonder on the train, will they or won't they meet again?

A month after I return from my trip I receive a letter from Odile. It answers the question as to whether or not she and Irena would meet up again:

Dear Alison, I thought you'd like to know that I finally got a letter from Irena. I'm enclosing a Xerox so that you can enjoy her idiomatic English. Obviously, Alison, we'll be seeing each other again. And probably again after that. Maybe one of these days I may actually come out of the closet at work. Odile.

Irena's note reads:

Dear Odile! I am back from Crimea. It is a very beautiful place, the Crimea. If I didn't know Russian it would have been impossible. Sometimes on a long day in the Crimea I remember our walk at the North Sea. I remember slowly we climbed to the hill, in the mean time with a short rest. We've making good time. At the moment we climbed speechless forward, above us the clear blue sky, around us the quietly of the forest, our lips oftener and oftener soundlessly moved to each other. The trail wasn't a suitable place for making love, we had to continue the walk. And then you asked me to come to you and led me higher into the sand. You pulled with a slow-lowly moment my trousers, my shirt out. So I stood there naked. You sat down. And looked at me naked bottom as though there was a note of a million. Then you did your palms flat over my eyes kissing me and kissing everywhere. My blood ran faster. It was love as if the breeze put me on the clouds. You told me your wish to lick me especially on this path. It was no obstruction from my side. You put your head between my legs and started me high and low lick. It seemed I was in round about. I shouted. You was the best licker in the North Sea sand and on this earth. O, goodness, it was nice. I lost all sense of shame. At this moment I am again very busy with my two new paintings, indeed with same theme she-she. It's going

very well. Odile, it's incredible, I use other colors, I am very sur-
prised about it, when I watch my paintings. I hope you will see it
over when you finally again here! Will you come? Take care of
your self. Love yours Irena.

I return the double letter to its envelope and slip it into file
folder number two.

"I feel like a virgin"

I n Greece, I travel to a house on a small island I've visited again
and again through the years. The light beguiles. On my way
back from a swim—yes, the swimming goes on into December
sometimes—I pass a man and a woman I've casually known for
many years—Maggie Martin, a former dancer originally from Jamaica, and Stathe Dekavallas, a retired Greek architect. They're
known on the island for their operatic relationship. They have
their arms snaking around each other, swaying slightly from side to
side as they walk in the direction of their seafront villa. They hail
me, explaining that they've had too much wine at lunch because
they're celebrating.

"I feel so strange," Maggie comments, after kissing me on both
cheeks in a queenly gesture. "I feel like a virgin."

I do a double take. I know that Maggie has been married at least
two times before, has a grown daughter and grandchildren, and
that Stathe has two children past university age.

"A virgin?"

"Something like that. You see, Stathe got his divorce last week. From the time he got his divorce, Alison, I express to you I haven't made love to him. It's so strange to be with a man who doesn't belong to someone else. After sixteen years of being the other woman, I'm with a man who's free. I feel shy like a virgin."

I am so struck by this comment that I ask if they'd be willing to be interviewed. They agree and we make an appointment. Still entwined, they stagger on. I hope they'll remember our appointment. They do. A few days later, I join them in their living room facing the spangled sea at sunset. The spectacle is over, the sun has sunk below the hills and the last lights from it—yellows, pinks, the palest blue—are draining away. On the walls are wonderful paintings, mostly landscapes, done by local artists. Maggie places a teak tray of drinks, teas and biscuits before us. I bring up the comment that had intrigued me so, while Stathe lights a fire in the stone hearth. The temperature is dropping now that the sun's gone.

"The other day you told me that you felt like a virgin. Can you explain this?"

There is a long pause. She sips from a tall glass of something that looks like iced tea but, knowing Maggie, probably holds a shot or two of vodka as well. She's thin as a rake, ageless. Her ochre sibyl's eyes draw mine.

"I'm finally living with a man that's not married."

She chuckles, sips from her glass.

"It's easy when you're living with a man that's married and you can be a little diva . . . a devil. Right now I have to face our reality and—it was really crazy—I had to put him away and then retake him as a single man. It's not logical. It's only sentimental. It isn't that I'm a virgin. I want to feel like a virgin again, like an innocent

girl just beginning her journey. I think it's only me who would react this way."

This makes more sense.

"Why?" I ask Stathe. "Why divorce after all this time?"

"As we are growing older and older, so we have to put this reality of ours into practicality."

"You always look so happy when I run into you. So in love."

He's compact and wily, has dark, unruly hair, sad eyes.

"We *are* happy. Bitterly happy," he replies. "I've lived with Maggie now for sixteen years without being married. But it took a long,
long time to get my divorce. We came together in 1988. I must tell
you, I'm very much to the exotic. I'm bored with the white color
and have a penchant to an erotic wife, to have attention to people
who have another color. I saw her . . ."

"Where?"

"In a beauty salon. I said, 'Wow!' We didn't talk, we just . . ."

". . . we nodded." Maggie finishes the sentence, Stathe starts a
new one. "Then about ten years later, I would say, we met again at
a taverna. I had just decided to separate from my wife, to resign
from my job. Yes. I was really tired and bored. I'd already realized
that I'm playing my life like a role in the theater. Not living it. I decided just to change everything at any cost. Maggie was at the same
stage for her own reason. She had just walked away from . . ."

". . . everything had collapsed under me."

"I saw her and wanted to catch her. Or to die, at least. But Maggie was at the end of something . . ."

She interrupts, "I had to be careful. My eight-year relationship
with a German was not quite finished. So I was careful. We took off
to other places. We went to the island of Aegina. We made mad

rendezvous in the island of Spetsei and like places. Finally he was forced to tell his wife about us."

"My wife asked me, 'I heard from my friend that you are with Maggie. Is it something serious?' I said yes."

She challenges him with her musical, yet steely tone of voice.

"I didn't believe it was *that* serious."

"For me it was."

To Maggie: "What did you think it was, a lighthearted interlude or . . . ?"

"No. We shared wonderful evenings. He didn't speak English, I was teaching him English. I really didn't know how I felt until I knew that I'd finished with my last husband. Then I knew that this was it."

I ask for a little background. Stathe explains that he came from a family that was created between two refugees from Smyrna who were thrown out by the Turks in 1922. The family came to Greece penniless, with nothing.

Maggie adds, "They walked here."

"We were an immigrant family that flourished. I studied architecture and then worked in the civil aviation with aerodromes. After twenty-five years, I wanted to change the totality of my life."

Maggie was a young girl when Jamaica got its independence in 1963. Her parents took her away to England, where her father was secretary to the ambassador.

"My father was a great bon vivant. He got into debt. By the way, my mother's family is still in Jamaica. I grew up and finished school in England, at Chelsea High School, living in Redcliff Gardens. My father was a great man. In England he changed 380 degrees, stopped being a bon vivant, became a family man, took care of us. I was studying dance at the London Academy of Dance. Classical dance, ballet, until I was chosen to be part of an exchange with Alvin Ailey. Alvin Ailey got interested in me and so I joined a group. I was taught primitive dancing for the first time. I was seventeen. A few of us formed a group and went to Switzerland. There were seventeen in the group. Five boys, twelve girls. I was seen by a modeling agency and, though I continued dancing, I began modeling."

She explains that at that time she got pregnant and had her daughter, whom she named Simone.

"The modeling agency got into deep shit. I had some money so I took over the agency. When Simone was three and a half years old her father reappeared and we married."

Talking about the past causes her to tear up. "Oh boy, this is hard. At the time, I was number one as the little colored girl in Geneva."

She's quite emotional. I ask Stathe, "So here we are, a few years later. Let me ask you, Stathe, I heard you had some health problems a few years ago."

"I think it was a depression. It happened in '96 and it happened for the reason that, I think, it was the first time I started thinking about making another change in my life, to get the divorce. I talked to my wife and she put down her conditions. Also there were some financial fears. Then I had a very, very hard attack of a disc. I got an operation in July of '96. I was not feeling strong."

"Papa, the physical healing was so fast. It was what happened mentally after."

"Okay. It was. The operation made my body feel not so strong. I'd been an athlete. I'd been a very powerful being."

He tears up.

"From '89 on I was giving three quarters of my income to my wife and daughter. My son was already at university with a scholarship. I was brought up by my parents to be . . . ha, ha . . . responsible and . . . ha, ha . . . guilty. I'm still like that. My depression lasted four, maybe five months. Then I got out of it."

"Did you ever seek help?"

"I went to a psychiatrist."

"Do you know what got you out of it?"

"I know but it doesn't matter."

Maggie disagrees. "It does. It's that I had been watching you pacing, not eating, not sleeping, losing a kilo every day. He didn't talk to me. We were sleeping together, he never touched me, we just slept. Then one day I realized I couldn't live in the situation. I told him, 'You know what. I'm going away.' He said, 'You can't do that.' I pulled off a belt and I beat him. I beat him and I beat him very gently, and the next day we talked: I said, 'Now that I've given you the spanking for what you did to me, are you going to tell me what is wrong?' He said to me, 'I can't stand being rent . . . living in the house of someone else in Athens.'"

Me, bemused: "Renting?"

Stathe: "Yeah. Yeah. I had a hundred million drachma, something like that, from land I'd just sold, but I didn't own our apartment."

Maggie: "I said, 'Now you go and find us an apartment. I'm going to the island.' I came here. Three days later he called. He said, 'I have something to show you.' He was walking. He was talking. He was driving."

"So it just lifted? Life's a miracle."

Maggie: "By taking action instead of wallowing in shit. But it was my belt. I still have the belt downstairs."

Stathe: "You are lying. You hit me with the telephone. Broke it."

Maggie: "I have the belt downstairs that I whipped you with."

Stathe: "I would like you to do it now."

I suggest: "You can start a therapeutic community. All the people with depression will come . . . the belt and the therapy. They'll be cured. I'm joking."

Stathe: "One thing I must say with Maggie. We came together from '89. I was dealing with a person who has much anger. She sometimes went into very, very, very violent things with her ex. They beat each other and went to court. On top of that, she was drinking like hell."

I wait but he says nothing more so I address my question to Maggie: "Do you think fights are good or bad for a relationship?"

"I don't know if they're good or bad. All I know is if there's a piece of shit there . . . can I be naughty now? It's like going to the toilet and you can shit but there's one little piece left. Those fights in a relationship are like that. One little piece of shit. You're so happy you've gotten rid of the rest, but there's one little thing there, and you can't be comfortable until you sit on the toilet again."

Maggie and Stathe

"Sitting on the toilet is the fight?"

"Yeah."

"So fights have an end?"

Stathe pipes up, "They have an end. They have an end."

I ask Maggie: "You don't dig your heels in?"

"No, no. We have never for one second. Even last night we

were sitting here and we were having a few drinks and going blah blah blah and I said to him, 'Just give me time to accept this.' I said, 'Look, stupid, it just takes me time.'"

"And you still feel like a virgin?"

She nods.

They walk me outside to the terrace that's drenched with moonlight. There are bright stars above and we hear the whooshing sound of the sea spilling against the rocks. The nutlike smell of smoke from burning olive wood rises from theirs and other chimneys, is in the air. Stathe puts his arms around Maggie.

"She's a child in many ways, you know. This is what I like about her . . . love about her. But she's a fucking child. We are together every moment."

Maggie adds, "Three hundred sixty-five days a year, twenty-four hours a day."

"Even though you've willed yourself a virgin once again?"

"Something like that. It's a new beginning. It's happened and we're okay. I don't want to marry Stathe because it's what I should do. I really mean this from the bottom of my heart. I want to marry him because I want to marry him."

Maggie plants a set of kisses on my cheeks. Stathe does too. Before I go, he adds, "I remember a little poem of my mentor George Seferis. It is called 'Confession.' It goes something like: '*We spend all the night arguing and fighting and there's nothing left for us but waiting for a blessing.*'" He laughs like a naughty boy. "I got the blessing."

Homecoming

While scrambling eggs, tomatoes and feta cheese for break-fast, I turn on the radio. Rather than Greek news or bouzouki music, I hear lines from the old Stevie Wonder song "Yes-terday." Without thinking, I begin to sing along: *What happened to / The world we knew . . . Yester-Me, Yester-You, Yesterday.* The song is followed in quick succession by Roy Orbison's "It's Over" and Jane Olivor's "Whispering Grass Don't Tell the Trees." Easily over-riding the passage of time, these songs immediately return me to old places, smells and tastes, to the good times I have spent with old friends and, of course, the great loves of my life.

One of my clipped wedding announcements from the *New York Times* comes to mind: The woman's name, Katherine Emmet, age fifty-four, the man, James Peterson, fifty-six. They met (and remet) on a bus that was traveling to Vermont where they both had sec-ond homes. They began to date, and swam together at a public pool. Then they were married in St. Paul's Chapel on Broadway and Fulton Street. Mr. Peterson describes what happened this way:

> *. . . Falling in love and getting engaged and marrying in your 50's is somewhat akin to rereading the great literature you read at 18.*

Just as I'm about to sit down and eat, the radio begins to play Middle Eastern music My sense of being out on the limb of midlife, with no points of reference, returns.

"I felt I'd known her all my life and she felt she'd known me all her life"

Later in the morning, on another part of the island, Mary Calothis nee Gladstone tells me:

"I had been three years in a single bed and after some months of conducting a new love affair on it, I decided to order a double bed. Because the new mattress was so large, Panayiotis, who transported it from the harbor on his pony, had to take the long route round by the sea to get to the house. That was the easy part. We then had to maneuver it through the narrow door and push and heave it up the very steep narrow staircase to my room. Its arrival could not have been worse timed, as my lover had just walked out on me. But I think you should speak with Tony first; he's outside on the terrace."

She's speaking about Tony Church, an English stage actor

who'd been having an affair with a Greek anthropologist named Christina and had decided to study Greek. He's long and lean, with a sculpted jaw. Each word he speaks in his deep voice resonates as if he were reciting Shakespeare. I go out and join him on a tiny back terrace, and we drink cold juice in wineglasses.

"I was beginning to see some sort of retirement looming. Not my style. Old actors never retire. I could not envisage a life of idleness hanging around Christina. The thought would have been horrifying to her and we'd become scratchy in our last holiday together. I decided to learn Greek."

The teacher who'd been recommended to teach him Greek was Mary.

"I was told, 'Go down the road from the Four Corners shop, toward the little harbor, and you'll find some steps; then look for the last building with a blue door.' Somehow I found it, knocked and was admitted up a very steep flight of internal stairs to a wondrous room with windows open on three sides. Mary, hair turning gray, spectacles on her nose, gave me a big, friendly smile. She had dancing blue-gray eyes."

He stops to wet his lips with juice.

"I decided to begin my lessons while I was waiting for the part of Ulysses in *Tantalus* to be enlarged and sent to me so I could read it. I'd been having eye problems—macular degeneration—and couldn't read ordinary print anymore. *Tantalus* is a huge, epic play."

It would be staged in Denver, where, for fifteen years, Tony had been head of the master of fine arts acting program at the Denver Center for the Performing Arts.

"Looking back, I realize that I was ready to fall totally and completely in love with somebody I would want to spend every minute of my life with. As you know, that turned out to be Mary."

He laughs wryly.

"Mary may regret the 'every minute' part of it. I think things started with the fact that we're both very, very English. There were so many things we shared. Having spent all those years in Denver, I had not been in the company of English people for a long time."

I asked what kinds of things he and Mary shared.

"Oh . . . childhood games, camping, making what we call dampers, where you get a green stick, make a fire and lump of dough that you push on the stick and hold over the fire."

"We called them doughboys when I was a Girl Scout."

"We both come from the southeast of England. Many things in that part of that world stand still. The more we talked about it, the more my childhood and hers got increasingly alike. Extraordinary. This was totally untrue of my relationship with any other woman. My first wife came from the north of England, very practical North Country."

Feathery clouds tinged with violet float tranquilly across the sky. Mary and I sit outside on another terrace on another day. She mentions their similarities too.

"When Tony and I went out for the first time, I was a little bit nervous. He was very attentive and wanted to know about my life. Everything I mentioned he had some connection with. Immediately there came a feeling of, well, the whole relationship with Tony is about coming home. He said he's never had that feeling with anyone in his life. It's absolutely true of me as well. It's the girl next door. It's a coming home completely internally, finally finding someone who understands the creative, artistic process as well. It allows one freedom."

"May I ask how old you were when you met Tony?"

"I must have been fifty-two at the time. Yes. He's seventy-four now, so he was seventy. He had just had his seventieth birthday. He was on a high and I was on the lowest low. He'd had his birthday and been fêted. He'd come from doing six weeks of a solo show of his own creation, which had played to packed houses in Denver to a public which adores him."

"Shakespeare?"

A tiger cat lands on the terrace wall with a soft thud and eyes us distrustfully.

"Not exactly. The show was called *Give 'Em a Bit of Mystery*. It is about the history of Shakespearean acting and actors from as far back as we know them in 1606, up to the present day to Judi Dench. It's delightful. In retrospect, I realize Tony needed something to fill the void after such an intense experience. By the way, I'd been divorced from my Greek husband Aris a while at this point. I also had been dumped by a lover. The lover was someone else. Tony was in a relationship with Christina then which, although he didn't realize it, was beginning to fade."

"How long had you been married to Aris?"

"We'd known each other since I was eighteen. We'd passed twenty-five years of marriage. That's a very long time. Happily, though, we're on friendly terms."

"He's your act one."

"Absolutely. He was the first man I made love with. That's huge. I left him in 1996 and met Tony in 2000."

Back to Tony:

"What were you like at twenty-five?"

"At twenty-five years old I didn't think of getting married at all."

"Why was that?"

"I don't know. I felt I was never going to be someone who could settle down with a woman. I was not confident with women."

"But by the time you met Mary, you'd had a lot of experience with women."

"Quite. And of course I did marry at age twenty-eight."

"How long was it from the first Greek lesson until you fell in love with Mary?"

"Four or five days."

Mary is somewhere inside the house. Tony calls out. His actor's voice projects as if he's speaking lines from *Hamlet*.

"Mary! How many lessons did I have from you before it happened? Four?"

There's no reply, so we walk into the house together and find Mary in her studio.

"Was it after the fourth lesson that we knew?"

"I think it was more than that."

"How many more?"

"It was the eighth, the tenth. Yes. Yes. Yes."

"There you are. I know it was damn quick."

Back to Mary:

"When I left Aris, I saw the light. I know what that expression really, really means, because something just went *ping* and that was it. In an instant. Of course it had been bottling up. There was a feeling of rightness with Tony. I suppose it wasn't a flash in the same way. We met on September fourth. The following weekend Christina came to stay with Tony at her *spitaki* ['little house' in Greek], and they invited me for Sunday brunch. I felt really at home and found Christina extremely interesting."

Because she'd been welcomed by both of them at brunch, she didn't have any misgivings about accepting Tony's invitation to eat out one evening, a few days after Christina had gone back to Athens.

"We had such a good time that night, so we decided to try another taverna two nights later. After that meal we *knew*. When we left this taverna, which now doesn't exist, we left hand in hand and by the next day we'd become lovers."

"Quite."

"Tony had only three weeks more before he was due in England to start rehearsing *Tantalus*. In that time he announced to his family that he'd met *the* woman. You see we both knew. It sounds quite crazy for a seventy-year-old."

"How quickly did Tony tell Christina?"

"He was going to put it off. She came over for the weekend. He took her out for a meal to a small fishing village nearby. At the end of the meal, Tony just said, 'I've met someone.' And Christina said, 'It's Mary, isn't it?' 'Yes,' he confessed. They took a boat back in silence. When they got up to her house she said, 'Well, you'd better go to her.' That night I had a friend visiting, and we were eating down at Captain George's taverna. Suddenly this distraught figure appears, and announces, 'She chucked me out. I've got nowhere to go.' More or less. Anyway, we sat him down and got him a drink. He came straight back with me to my flat after the meal."

"Did you ever have the sense when you were twenty, twenty-five, that you'd met *the* person?"

"No. Every day at breakfast we still say, 'Wow!' When we're looking at the moon, we say, 'Thank God we decided. Thank God we followed through, that we really knew it was right.' Absolutely."

Right before the wedding, they told their Greek-American best man—Nick—that they were going to speak lines from *As You Like It* at the ceremony. They asked Nick to translate; they wanted him to speak the lines in Greek following the lines in English since many of the guests would be Greek. Nick agreed, made the translations and during the solemnizing ceremony stood behind Tony. Max, Tony's grandson, acted as ring bearer, holding the ring on a handmade little pillow. All three of Tony's grown children were in attendance, as was one of Mary's two sons.

The ceremony was brief:

Tony: "To you I give myself, for I am yours."
Mary: "To you I give myself, for I am yours. Wedding is great Juno's crown, O blessed bond of board and bed."
Tony: "'Tis Hymen peoples every town. High wedlock then be honored."
Tony and Mary: "Honor, high honor and renown. To Hymen, god of every town."

Almost a year has passed since the wedding. Tony and Mary had just returned to the island when I again talk with them. I sit across from them at their kitchen counter. The sky is pale blue.

Tony informs me, "I'd had a heart attack in Denver. I don't know if you knew it."

I did know.

"Knowing I had only so much time, I was glad Mary and I had acted quickly."

"What now?"

"He just turned down an invitation by Peter Hall to play . . ."

". . . the part of Old Adam in the first half of *As You Like It*. A lovely part and a small part which Shakespeare himself is supposed to have played. At first I thought it would be possible. Then I realized I didn't have the confidence even to manage that, or the right to drag Mary all around England and the United States, taking her away from her own work. So we are here for good."

Mary: "Love's a full-time business now. It never seemed to me a full-time business before."

Me: "So you've totally consolidated your new life. Together. Legally. Facing the future. A few nice friends. Harmony with ex-spouses? Children?"

Tony: "Yes."

Me: "So you've left no smashed baggage?"

Mary: "I don't think so. That's all been tidied up. Tony's doing his memoirs and I'm painting."

Before Tony ran the school in Denver he'd run a drama school in England. He'd also acted with the Royal Shakespeare Company, had always been a working actor. At one time or another he's played seventy-six roles in Shakespeare.

I ask him, "What has Shakespeare to say about love later in life?"

"It's very interesting. There are many different love affairs in Shakespeare, developed in many different ways. But, always it seems to me, the declaration of love, when it comes, it comes with such openness and possessiveness that the other person has to do something about it quickly. In *Romeo and Juliet*, it's immediate. One dance, that's it. I didn't believe I would ever really fall in love that way. The suddenness . . . *falling* in love . . . *falling* . . . not catching someone but *falling*. Is it falling into love? It seems to me, what happened with Mary and me, is we both fell *into* love, fell into each other, from different places. There's no doubt about it."

"You mean you knew the exact instant you fell in love?"

"Oh, absolutely."

Mary nods in agreement.

"Do you remember the moment, did your eyes meet?"

"At one of those first meals we were talking more and more about things we shared across this extraordinary eighteen-year divide. I felt I'd known her all my life and she felt she'd known me all her life. I suddenly thought, What am I wasting my time about? This is it. And I said it, and she said, 'Yes, it is.' "

He covers both her hands with his elegant hands.

"There's only one romantic couple in Shakespeare of any age, and that's Antony and Cleopatra."

"Are they midlife?"

"Oh, absolutely midlife. Cleopatra was, I think, what would be called very midlife in those days—late forties. And Antony was the same age—over fifty. It's a play about middle-aged love. She's a jealous woman, an excitable, fiery woman, and he is, by nature, more of a plodder. They're wonderfully depicted with wildly different natures. One absolutely generous to a fault, open, romantic; and the other is totally practical. You know from the minute they meet that disaster is going to come."

"The disaster?"

"Suddenly he breaks away, she insists he stay in Egypt. But in the end, they're together and they win. Because it's the only case in Shakespeare where you have middle-aged lovers, they always cast someone who is a big symbol of virility in the theater or film. The best performance of that play I've ever seen is by Anthony Hopkins and Judi Dench. Judi Dench was fifty when she played it. She became fifty while she was playing it. Judy remains incredibly attractive, exciting to this day. It was magic."

Wedding of Tony and Mary

We begin to look at the wedding photos.

"Do you think it's just good fortune that you found each other?"

Mary replies, "I think luck comes into it. Things happen by just letting go."

"What do you mean?"

"Letting go of struggling to make something work that doesn't. Like my marriage. Letting life tell me."

The photos underscore her words.

A fter I'm back in New York, I get the following e-mail from Mary:

Tony's ex-wife Margaret is on her way back to London having had a marvelous time here. The highlight of her stay was a trip on Aris's boat. I opted out, but Margaret, Aris and Tony had a great time, captained by Aris. It was strange, to say the least, mulling over wedding photos in Margaret's presence just like we did with you. "Very Noel Coward" a friend remarked. It's a relief to have the visit over. Lots of love, Mary.

"We're the same and we change"

I am sitting at a kitchen table in the small house in Greece with Marianne Christine Ihlen; Marianne is a sweet Norwegian woman with a round face, an opulent body, platinum white hair. I read from Jane Juska's book about sex rediscovered, A *Round-Heeled Woman*.

> *A long time later, months later, when I was able to think about Jonah and me without cringing, without crying, I considered the matter of age and passion and desire. Jonah, I'd bet anything, wondered if he still could; I was a way of finding out. More than that, like me, he was looking for a place for his passion. The world has little use for us; we are old, what business have we with passion? So we found each other and who would know? Who would care? Old people, they should be dry. But we weren't.*

I watch her face for a response. She neither smiles nor frowns. Finally she speaks.

"I believe our sexuality never dies."

"Does sex still matter to you? Still interest you?"

"Yes! In many ways it is the most important energy we have. As a young woman with a young body, everything has to do with what the body looks like. Later we ask what the body feels like and wants. And thanks to my body work and meditation I come into contact with my sexuality/energy. I'm old. I have an old body. I'm seventy soon. What I see around is people who can't walk, can't do this and that anymore. I can still fly like a goat."

Marianne was born in Oslo, but grew up at her grandmother's house by the sea during the war.

"I was happy when I lived with Grandmother. I really do believe that she allowed me to live, to dream. We had a walk-in dollhouse, and she would visit me. We had dried green leaves for bread, stones for meatballs and potatoes. We drank water out of tiny little cups. She would walk out and say, 'Thank you for a delicious meal.' We slept in the same bed. Early in the morning, in winter, she put all my clothes under her body to make them warm. She died when I was eighteen. She once said to me, 'I know you will meet a man who speaks with a tongue of gold.' She was right."

The men in the first act of Marianne's life were writers, painters and poets. For these men—especially the two long-term relationships with men she refers to as "husbands"—she took on the role of Muse. The first husband was a well-known Norwegian novelist named Axel Jensen with whom she had her only child, also named Axel.

"Big Axel and I left Norway in 1958—he wanted to see the Oracle of Delphi. The first time I had the idea of myself as a Muse was when he sat in an Arab djelaba in front of his Remington typewriter and I went to the village to shop for green beans and potatoes. I got them going on the one burner so he had one meal a day. I would wash clothes and read all that he wrote. I was happy with that. I would sit with him, and he'd talk about Goethe and Jung and the universe. He was way out for the time. I had read Gurdjieff, Nietzche, Ovspensky from page one to two hundred fifty."

The man Marianne calls her second husband, though they were never legally married, was the Canadian poet and performer Leonard Cohen. He wrote the following about Marianne in one of his album jacket notes:

Marianne gave me many songs, and she has given songs to others too. She is a Muse. A lot of people I know think that there is nothing more important than making a song.

During an interview, Cohen expounded further on how Marianne's creative spirit inspired him: "It was really a great privilege to live in a house with her. It wasn't just that she was the Muse shining in front of the poet, she understood that it was a good idea to get me to my desk."

Marianne and Leonard lived together on and off during the sixties in a stone house on a Greek island. In still another interview, Cohen said of this time: "I found that my standard of living went down very sharply after I started to make money and become known. Before I had money I lived in a lovely white house on a Greek island. . . . With the advent of money I found myself spending more and more time in . . . taxis and airplanes and other unpleasant circumstances."

I ask Marianne, "The song that he wrote about you that is so well-known with the chorus—*Now so long, Marianne, it's time that we began, to laugh and cry and laugh about it all again*—what do you think about that?"

"It's a beautiful song, but the title originally was 'Come On Marianne.' 'Bird on the Wire' is really my song. That's when I got Leonard back to his desk again."

I serve her a glass of wine, then I bring a plate of feta cheese and black olives to the table.

"Have an olive."

"No, thank you," Marianne says as she stuffs two olives into her mouth, making us both crack up.

"You're like me. You have no willpower."

"Yes."

"You were speaking about the song 'So Long, Marianne.'"

"The many other songs that were written to me, no one else would know because they don't have my name on them. I've kept that time private. I've been approached by journalists, by magazines, by radio, and by television. I've never appeared, never accepted anything, never answered their questions."

"Good for you."

"Until today. There are things written about me but I had no part in it. I'm rather proud of my silence, of course. I was part of Leonard's secret life. I knew better than to have babies with him."

"Why?"

"I couldn't give him Jewish babies. After Greece I went to New York. I got mugged in a doorway, faced a knife this size, on the Lower East Side, on Clinton Street. Axel went to P.S. 27. Leonard and I were drifting apart. He was starting to get very famous at the time. He was being pulled into quite another world. I didn't go there with him. He saw me, he saw me . . ."

"He discovered you? Created you?"

"No, no. I mean he saw *me*. He saw my value."

I drizzle olive oil onto the chunk of feta and sprinkle a bit of fresh oregano over it, then refill Marianne's glass.

"During these Muse decades, I lived in Greece, New York, Mexico and Norway. There were many men beside Axel and Leonard. I was a lonely mother. I wanted someone to share . . ."

She doesn't finish the sentence. We're quiet for a moment, listening to the island's sounds of crowing roosters, braying donkeys, of birds, the soft *putt-putt* of small fishing boats. After twenty years abroad, Marianne returned home to Oslo. As it turned out, she didn't bring her Muse's identity with her.

"Had you tired of being a muse? Were you looking for something different in love? Partnership perhaps?"

"I had no job. No money. I wanted to be independent. Yeah, I really mean it. I still want to be independent. At the time my son, Axel, was sixteen, seventeen, going to gymnasium. I was middle-aged. I had to find a job. After all these days in dreamy places . . . when you live in a dream . . . when you run around for twenty years sitting at the poet's feet, to be a secretary in an oil-drilling company with engineers building platforms in the North Sea . . . that's where I ended up. At first, my new identity became secretary at an oil-drilling company and then wife and mother."

She laughs gayly.

"It's not to be laughed at."

"You're right. It's honorable work, an honorable life. We have to wake up, pay the rent. After all those years of travel, I knew nobody. My friends from the past lived such different lives, so it was hard. They had cars, garages and diamond rings, or they were already divorced three times. I was very lost when I first came back. Very lost. Very lost."

She spears a chunk of feta with a fork.

"In the midst of all these engineers, I saw this tall, dark and handsome man named Jan. There was something about him. I was fascinated by the intricate, technical drawings, that he could transform them into a drilling platform. He invited me to dinner. We went out with his friends. We went back to Jan's flat. And I never left. I left the next morning to go to work of course but— metaphorically—I never left. His marriage was over two years before I met him. There were three daughters, the youngest was nine and lived with the mother. Jan is an engineer with a strong spiritual longing. A pillar, I tell you."

"This falling in love with Jan, did you have a sense of destiny about him like you had about the others—the men with tongues of gold?"

"Destiny. Destiny, what does it really mean? I was back home in Norway and I couldn't find a better man, a better companion, a better partner. My mother loved him, kept saying, 'Why didn't you marry him to begin with? This is the man.' He was there for everybody and my son Axel too. A load was taken off my shoulders. We had a wonderful time together, lots to share. We got married.

"I think part of it was that we had so much to talk about. He had a tough life, a fantastic life, and I had had a life he didn't know existed. Thinking back, there never was a dull moment."

Wedding of Marianne and Jan

Marianne and Jan have been married for twenty-three years.

"When I first returned home after my youthful years of travel, when the glitter of my life abroad dissipated, I experienced some emotional rawness. At one point I tried therapy, but realized it wasn't for me. Then I met Jes Bertelsen and his wife, Hanne Kizach, who started Vaekstcentret—the Center of Work, Growth and Meditation—in Denmark. They gave me the 'tools' through working, among other things, with body therapy, breathing exercises and meditation."

"Oh!"

"I had a lot to sort out to get to the core of myself. It gave me strength to help my son Axel, who unfortunately at the age of fifteen, during his first meeting with his father, was given LSD and got very sick. What had we done to these sensitive children in those early years of drugs and alcohol?"

Marianne pours herself another glass of wine. Someone in the neighborhood is listening to bouzouki music a little too loudly.

"Do you feel that you've been a muse to Jan?"

"Not in the way I once was. We have supported each other, have met somehow with our individual 'luggage' and grown with every difficulty solved."

"And love in this second part of your life? Sex?"

"Love somehow gets deeper the more you work with yourself. And sex in all forms will grow."

I read a quote from a book titled *Leonard Cohen—In His Own Words*:

At the age of 50 all you feel is a certain kind of strength, just the strength to go on, deeply. The heart becomes truly passionate as you get older and it gives you the deepest kind of appetite for everything.

The features of her face soften.

"He's still my favorite poet, him and Seferis, the Greek. I love short poems, Japanese haiku. Knut Hamsun started me off. If you read German you should read Hamsun in German. In love, though, I don't think it has anything to do with a man all the time. I think it has something to do with knowing yourself, being able to stand your own company, being at home with yourself. I have a way to go but I don't have to change partners anymore. I think it's much more interesting to work it out. Can't we change love to compassion? For the last twenty years I've walked in the Dalai Lama's footsteps. If the world were Buddhist, we would have compassion and not kill."

"You've stuck together, you and Jan. Do you love him as much as you did?"

"That changes too . . . love. In Norwegian—it doesn't translate into English well—we have a word that means too much in love when you meet. It's *forelsket*—too much love. Then after some time that is transformed into love."

"You mean lower the flame? Is that a good image?"

"*Ja*. You learn to accept and forgive. We're the same and we change. I had been back in Greece many times and have met Leonard many times. Some years ago when I was in Greece, Leonard invited me to his—our—house for dinner. He had just returned from India. It was pouring rain, and I looked like a drowned cat when I arrived. We shared a little meal that his maid had prepared."

She gestures gracefully with her arms and hands.

"I watched him moving. I keep saying when people ask me— 'What is Buddhism?'—It's a way of life, not a religion. Seeing Leonard move . . . slow, he's so into everything he does . . . was like a meditation. He walked over, and he was doing the dishes, and I was sitting there looking at what had once been my little kitchen. Nothing was changed in the house we'd lived in together for so long. There was the same box with a young woman blindfolded playing a harp without any strings. The lid is so tight because it's rusted, you can't get it up. On the back a short poem I have forgotten. I saw that the Christ that someone had given him was gone. It was a beautiful wooden Christ, old and rotten. Christ had hardly any hands, the cross was rotten, no feet."

She touches my hand.

"But the church bell was still there, the one I'd brought with me when I moved in. He didn't remember how I came by it. I did. He asked me to tell him the story. This is the story: I was working on a private yacht in between my two marriages, and we anchored up in Santorini. When we visited the volcano at the edge of the crater, I sacrificed an old Egyptian scarab that my first husband had given me. Then we ended being invited to a local wedding in the village. In those days, a wedding lasted at least three days. Late at night I slipped away into the forest to pee. I looked down and something caught my eye. I used my sandal to pull away some grass and earth, and there was an old church bell. On one side was an imprint of the Madonna and the Child. First I'd sacrificed something from my first husband, and then I find a Greek Orthodox bell."

Suddenly the bouzouki music stops. There's silence until we hear the sound of a small owl.

"When I moved into Leonard's house many years later, I brought it with me. When I left, I left the bell. After I reminded him, Leonard said, 'I'm happy that you told me the story because I'd forgotten about the bell.' He walked over to the sink and finished the dishes, and I was sitting there still looking around my little kitchen in which nothing had been changed. I felt so calm and so relieved. I had no wish to go back in time. It was a very, very beautiful meeting. Next morning we met for coffee at Tassos coffee shop on the port."

The sun begins to pour into the kitchen in an uncomfortable way so I get up and close the yellow shutters.

"Earlier I had come back to Greece with the Swedish author named Goran Tunstrom and his wife, the painter Lena Cronqvist. Swedish TV was making a documentary about Goran's life and work. We all stayed at Leonard's house. I knew Goran from way back when he first came to Greece in 1959. One night they filmed during dinner at Old Duskos taverna. I will send you a copy of this documentary. Goran appears with his grilled fish and cats at his feet. You zoom down, there are fifteen cats at his feet. The camera zooms down at the cats and then back at the table where you see us and hear me saying, 'Before I sat at the poet's feet. Now I sit at the poet's table.' "

She takes a mouthful of wine.

"That's where the thing has changed. In act one I sat at the poet's feet, now I sit at his table . . . I sit at your table."

Marianne takes another olive.

I ask, "Do you look like your father or your mother?"

"My mother. She had a sort of Mongol face. That's why I've always looked down because I thought my face was too round. My first boyfriend used to say, 'Have you lost something, Marianne?' My father was fifty-seven when he died. He was a poet at heart. My mother was scared and spoiled and came out rough and tough just to survive, always finding something wrong with me, with my hair, with my way of dressing. She thought I lived in a sleeping bag in Greece. But before she died she had to 'let go' and thanked me for visiting her and bringing wine and fruit."

Our glasses are empty.

"Jan and I were with her the night she died in September. She would have been ninety-four in April and she spent the eleven last years in an old woman's home. She didn't enjoy the first six years. On the night she was dying, I could find no peace in bed. I got dressed and asked Jan to take me there, just as my mobile rang and the message was: 'I think our mother is going.'"

I ask if she'd like more wine; she shakes her head no.

Marianne at seventy

"I was grateful to find a doctor who knew my mother, to tell him to help her, that I didn't want her to have any pain. 'Guaranteed!' he said. He saw her first. Then we went in. This was about one-thirty at night. She died about six in the morning. Through the night we talked to her and, together, we read poems and laughed. She was conscious but could not speak. I thanked her and we talked about all the fun and all the good dinners she had made for us. I thanked her for being so strong through life. We held her hands and wet her mouth. I opened the window and told her to fly out. Thank God we knew that hearing is the last that goes, that dies. Now I am the oldest one in the family. Nobody should die in pain; nobody should have to die alone. If possible, we should all die in our own bed at home."

She begins to gather her things to leave.

"I found a beautiful picture of my mother as a little girl with curly hair set in a golden frame. When I look at the picture I know, even my mother was once a little girl. We have all been little girls with curls. I can forgive my mother, I can forgive myself. Acceptance and forgiveness. Acceptance and forgiveness."

If music be
the food of love,
play on.

"*Perhaps Lila and I are two halves*
of the same whole, reunited?"

Though the days are short, they're beautiful. The end of the year is divine in Greece, and the light changes every day; but soon it will be time to leave the island. Because every swim might be the last at this time of year, there's poignancy in each. The days are shortening, the light is captivating against the dappled Peloponnesian hills every time I swim out into the salty sea. Because the Aegean is so buoyant, it is a pleasant place to bob and converse. The local jokester, nicknamed Thalia, whose eyes are black as olives, swims over and asks, "What are you writing these days? Another book about misery and war?"

I tell him.

"Ah! Sex and the elderly. I've got a story for you: Mr. Popidopolous hits seventy, and decides he wants to live a long time. He starts to diet and exercise, and gives up smoking. He loses his gut, his body firms up, and, to make the picture complete, he buys a toupee to cover his bald scalp. Then he walks out in the street and is hit by the first car that comes along. As he lies dying, he calls, 'God, how could you do this to me?' God answers, 'To tell you the truth, I didn't recognize you.'"

"That's not exactly what I'm looking for."

I notice a friend swimming my way. He's Pandias Scaramangas, an eighty-year-old Greek. Three years ago his wife Ileana died. Last year he married Lila, with whom he had had a secret relationship for at least twenty-seven years. I wave.

"Apropos of Pandias, here's one," Thalia gleefully says. "A woman in her late eighties goes to a doctor to complain about her husband's impotence. The doctor hears her out and asks, 'How old is your husband?' 'Eighty-eight.' 'When did you first notice his waning enthusiasm and inability to perform?' 'Well, the first time was last night, and again this morning.'"

Thalia breaks up over his own story. He's succeeded in getting me to crack a smile with this one. Pandias is beside us smiling his broad, ingratiating smile. Immediately this compulsive joke-teller pulls another joke from his quiver, aims and shoots:

"Three sisters, aged ninety-two, ninety-four and ninety-six, live in a house together. One night the ninety-six-year-old draws a bath. She puts her foot in and pauses. She yells to the other sisters, 'Was I getting in or out of the bath?' The ninety-four-year-old yells back, 'I don't know. I'll come up and see.' She starts up the stairs and pauses, 'Was I going up the stairs or down?' The ninety-two-year-old is sitting at the kitchen table, having tea listening to her sisters. After rapping on the kitchen table, she shakes her head and says, 'I sure hope I never get that forgetful, knock on wood.' She then yells, 'I'll come up and help both of you as soon as I see who's at the door.'"

Pandias drolly says, "What's this?"

Thalia tells Pandias, "She's writing about old age and sex."

We three tread water.

"And love?" asks Pandias.

Me: "Yes. And love."

I notice that, as time has passed, Pandias hasn't changed much physically.

"What does it all add up to?" he asks thoughtfully.

"What?"

"Love? Sex? Do you know that no one taught me anything about sex. One Italian woman I slept with said, 'Do this. Don't do that.' But no one ever taught me. If I am reincarnated, I'm going immediately to a sex school to learn techniques."

Thalia raises an eyebrow.

"I have much to say about love," Pandias tells me, so we make a date. Then I swim toward shore and leave him with Thalia, who's already starting another barrage of bad jokes.

One night there's a wild storm with Beaufort 8 winds—gale force—and pounding rains all flailing the bougainvillea and the geranium flowers on the terrace of the small house at which I'm staying. Twenty-four more hours of punishing winds and rains follow. Raging rivers flood down the stone steps from the mountains, walls wash away, cisterns overflow. It seems like the end of the world. Late Saturday night, the storm finally dies. The air is suddenly clear. Stars glint sharply. On Sunday morning, as usual, I hear the sound of roosters and I can once again see the faraway red light of the morning hydrofoil coming out of the darkness, blinking its way across the horizon.

Morning is fresh and beautiful. I, as well as everyone else, must begin cleaning up the mess left by the storm. I'm moved to notice among the trashed geraniums in their flooded pots, that—out of nowhere, unexpectedly, from twisting threadlike vines—periwinkle-blue morning glories have opened. They lift my spirits. They last the entire morning. By afternoon, the color begins to fade. By the time I'm due at my appointment, the petals have curled up.

Pandias and I sit in the study of his stone house. His new wife Lila is a patrician woman with the face of a Byzantine icon. Lila shuts the door behind her after bringing us a tray with coffee.

"I have the reputation of being a womanizer," Pandias confesses.

I already know this because I've known him a long time. He may be a bit of a rogue but he's got a good heart and has a long and intriguing amorous history. Doubtless there's much he has to say about love. We became acquainted a number of decades before at a wedding at which I'd been the maid of honor, and he'd been the best man. He had, in fact, provided the bridegroom with the suit he wore. In the intervening years, both of these friends—Anthony and Christina—had died hard deaths. For many years, when our paths crossed, because of the death of these friends, Pandias and I could hardly bear to speak to each other. When encountering each other we'd usually just shake our heads sadly. After the death of Pandias's wife, for some reason, we resumed our friendship.

He offers the platter of pastries. "Shall I give you a general outlook of my ideas on love?"

I shake my head yes.

"Both love and the development of the human brain go by waves, like the waves on the shore. One wave does not wait for the other to subside. One wave climbs over the other one while the other one is going away. Sometimes they synchronize well. You have one wave, one goes back, then you have the second. Very often, one wave falls onto another. And so you have turmoil, like in a mixer."

I'm listening.

"Sex is something that has to do with the lower layers of the brain. You have what they call the urge. Sex is like what reptiles do. They either attack or they withdraw. If they see something moving in a certain way, or smelling a certain way, they go toward it and want to unite with it. They want to become one. They want to embrace or be embraced by it."

His dark eyes twinkle with teasing and earnestness. He's about the same height as me, with the face of a friendly fox terrier. In spite of the show he makes of his chauvinism, he's beguiling and has always been generous to everyone.

"A higher part of the brain is mammalian. Mammals, say cats, they have urges, yes, but also instincts. When they have little babies they become tender, but if the gland secretes something else by mistake, this cat will eat her own kittens. Sex you get from the reptilian part of the brain. The second layer is love in a mammalian way, the mammalian part of the brain . . . affection, tenderness. The third layer of the brain is the neocortex, which means you think and calculate, so you marry a rich woman and get a dowry. These three layers of the brain very often do not mix harmoniously so you have someone who goes for sex to prostitutes, even though he loves his wife and children. Sometimes the three layers combine and you have someone who has good sex with his wife, he is tender with her, he thinks it's good socially, she's a nice person to go about with. But very often these things do not combine well and one is stronger than the other or fights it and drives you this way or that and makes you miserable. I like women more than men. I think most women are crazy and I think men are stupid and dull. I prefer crazy women to stupid men. I know that I'm stupid. That's the only thing I have in common with Socrates."

"You remarried recently. Looking at your life, this womanizing, what does love mean to you at this time?"

"Let me speak about sex first. The truth is that I never really liked sex very much nor felt skilled at it. For me sex was a way of approaching another person, getting to know. The best moment for me was afterward, when we smoked a cigarette and I'd ask her to tell me about her life, her first love and other stories."

I can't always tell when he's serious and when he's not.

"Sex—I considered even then, more so now—is a very stupid kind of motion. Going forward, backward, like an engine with a piston. Look at cats. Look at dogs. They all get a very stupid face while having sex. I had the urge for sex, so I wanted to do it and finish with it. To show off about it and get rid of the urge. I kept sex separate from other feelings. I would go to prostitutes. Often it was not a pleasant need but I had to do it. I love people but this is not sex. When I was young, I used to need it quite often. I know that wherever I go—you can parachute me into China—I'd find a woman who'll cook for me, who'll bring me coffee, or rather tea, and make love with me."

His eyes twinkle with naughtiness.

"How long were you married?" I ask.

His face saddens, tears fill his eyes.

"I was married for fifty years and I loved Ileana. I loved her. She was somehow my child. At the same time she kept me going because she had a lot of humor. She was very funny and extremely brave and very intelligent. More than me. I didn't know that until a friend heard me say that Ileana was stupid. He said, 'Be careful. She is more intelligent than you.' She was very, very special—half Greek, half Romanian."

He hands me a photo of a child about two years old.

"That's my granddaughter."

"What's her name?"

"Sophia."

It seems strange to me that a man who'd womanized throughout his married life would be so devastated by the death of his wife. It seemed like a contradiction. Perhaps because he's of another culture, of another generation, this grief is not a contradiction? It's something I can't explain, but so what. There is no doubt that his sad state is sincere and deep. He hands me another photo. This one is of himself with his arm around a beautiful woman, who looks like Louise Brooks. It's his wife, Ileana. He continues weeping.

"I knew when it was taken that it would be our last photograph together. I knew that I was going to die or she was. You can see it in the photo . . . we both felt it. What I imagined was dying first . . . me first."

A wash of tears rolls down his cheeks.

"We had two beds like this, facing each other, two separate rooms but we could see each other. I saw the trees moving with the air . . . the wind blowing the trees. I could see Ileana. I don't believe in afterlife. I don't believe in souls. Yet I know very often what's going to happen. I had an intuition that my and Ileana's son, Peter, would not live out his life, but I didn't worry about it because I figured by then they'll have the medicine he'd need. But Peter died of a brain tumor seventeen years ago. It happened, but without the medicine I hoped for."

"You went on, you continued living."

"Ah, yes."

"Did you think of suicide?"

"I want to commit suicide not for personal things but as a protest to this stupid universe that governs us, or rather for a cause that I cannot foresee yet. But I won't do it as it will anyway happen."

"Age? How do you feel about being eighty years old?"

"Awful. I didn't think it would happen to me. First of all, it's a shame to be old. It's a degradation. But you can't help it."

"I've known you for a long time. You look almost the same."

"Yes. But I looked like an old man when I was young. I've caught up with my face. I feel okay. It's just the shame of it. You feel you are disintegrating, every day a little more. You don't remember this or that. Every time I have to mention a name I have to wait five minutes to try to pry it up."

"Has your philosophy of life changed? Or are you the same as you were sixty years ago?"

"I've changed a lot. I've learned a lot of things. I wouldn't do the same mistakes. All my life has been a mistake. The only thing I haven't regretted is marrying Ileana and having Peter, even though he didn't stay long with us. Now I have Alexander, whom I had with Mireille."

Pandias and Mireille, a French woman, had had a long, tempestuous affair.

"She had a way of driving me crazy. I don't know if you can call it love. I became another person, aggressive, bad, crazy. I would say, 'Mireille, stop it! Stop it! I'm going to drive the car into the wall,' and she'd continue. Once I went full speed into a tree. We ended up in the hospital with broken limbs. Can you call that love?"

"The emotions were certainly strong."

"I said never again. I didn't know jealousy existed before that. Mammalian love is full of tenderness and looking after. But when jealousy enters . . . I think cats and dogs are very jealous. If you pet one the other will come."

He stands up, brushes crumbs off his shirt.

"Now we must go upstairs. Lila will get upset if I stay away much longer."

We walk up the stone stairway to the sitting/ dining room of his two-hundred-year-old house. The walls are decorated with large paintings, many of which he won at poker. Lila has set the table for lunch. She serves roast chicken with lemon sauce, roast po-tatoes and scoops of cool

Wedding of Pandias and Lila

lemon sorbet afterward. When the plates are removed, she spreads out a few photographs of their wedding on the table.

She tells me, "We were married one year ago in May . . ."

Pandias finishes the sentence, ". . . in Athens, a friend of mine was best man. A huge church in Kolonaki. The church was deco-rated with flowers as you see, but for another wedding."

Lila laughs and points out the various photos.

"We used their decorations. Lovely pink flowers. That's the priest. Those are Dutch people who had entered the church just to see it. They were happy to watch us get married, so they congratu-lated us."

Pandias puts his hand on Lila's shoulder.

"Zeus cut the original human in half and we're all looking to find the other half in order to become complete. The thing I like the most and agree with on human love is in Plato. Wait a minute."

He goes to his bookshelf and pulls out a dog-eared copy of

Plato's *Symposium*. It's in Greek with English translation on alternating pages.

"I want to find the place where Aristophanes tells Socrates . . . ah. . . ." He reads:

> . . . *the shape of each human being was a rounded whole, with back and sides forming a circle. Each one had four hands and the same number of legs and two identical faces on a circular neck. They had one head for both the faces, which were turned in opposite directions, four ears, two sets of genitals.*

I have to laugh. *Hedwig and the Angry Inch* comes to mind.

He explains: "You see Zeus found these beings overly strong and ambitious, too much competition to the gods. They were becoming too dangerous, too obnoxious. Zeus wondered, Should we kill them? Should we get rid of them? Instead, he said, 'Let's weaken them.'" He again reads:

> *Zeus . . . cut humans into two, as people cut sorb-apples in half before they preserve them or as they cut hard-boiled eggs with hairs. As he cut each one, he told Apollo to turn the face and the half-neck attached to it towards the gash. Zeus took pity on them and came up with another plan: he moved their genitals round to the front.*

"Perhaps Lila and I are two halves of the same whole, reunited?"

He smiles his devilish smile. Lila rolls her eyes, then brings a homemade cake from the kitchen and cuts it.

"Delicious," I comment, not lying, and ask Lila, "Where did you learn to cook?"

"I taught her," Pandias brags.

Lila nods her head. "I didn't even have a cooker in the house—nothing—when I met him. I couldn't even fry an egg. We'd always have lunch in restaurants."

"I bought her a book. The best investment I ever made."

"I learned for you. The first thing I did was a soufflé."

Me: "Was it a success?"

"Yes. But it was very well explained."

"You started then to cook for Pandias?"

"Yeah."

"When I met her she had never tasted fish."

"I didn't like it. But now I do."

To Lila: "What else did he teach you?"

Pandias answers for her, "Patience."

Lila answers for herself: "Many things."

To Lila: "What have you taught *him?*"

"To diet. To be healthy."

To Lila: "Do you depend on him?"

Pandias replies in her place: "She doesn't depend on me, I depend on her."

To Pandias: "Are you romantic?"

Pandias: "Not at all."

Lila: "You are."

We finish our cake and drink coffee.

"Years ago, I had another house on the island," Pandias explains. "I used to wake up early in the morning before the sun rose. I'd sit on the wall over there and wait for the sun to come up. I'd see the sun rise, would smoke my cigarette, read a little. I didn't know then that I was sitting beside the arch under what would one day be my house. One day I noticed the arch and thought, This is the house for me. It belonged to a German. He was desperate to sell it. He was selling it for one third of its price. Why? I asked him. He replied, 'Because next year I'm going to be fifty and I won't be able anymore to go up the hill.' I'm eighty," he chortles, "I go slowly, use a stick . . ."

Lila finishes his sentence, ". . . but he goes up and down the hill every day!"

A few days later, though I didn't know it at the time, turns out to be my last swim. Again that morning are newborn periwinkle-blue morning glories, their thin, curling vines wrapping themselves around the geranium stalks. What had been the surprise of a few morning glories that lived for one day only on the day after the big storm became a few more the next day. These also died. The day after that there were none. The following day—four. Every day I'd been given the gift of these heart-stopping blue petals and then the letdown as—through the day—they faded, curled, and died. Today there are ten dewy morning glories newly burst from their buds.

In the water I swim over to Lila and Pandias. We tread water and—I don't know why—the subject of death comes up.

Lila tells us: "Once I woke up, had hemorrhaged during the night. There I was, both me and my bedding soaked with blood."

I gasp. Pandias gapes at her as if he'd never heard the story. Her description of the bloody scene becomes more vivid. She describes the bright red stains on the sheets, on her nightdress. She concludes by saying, "But, do you know what? I felt an enormous sense of well-being. I'm not afraid of death, nor would I suicide for any reason."

Pandias agrees: "I doubt I'll ever commit suicide but if one chooses to die by one's own hand, I've been told one must eat a large quantity of good foie gras. Then one must drink a bottle of good champagne, wait one half an hour. Then . . . go into the sea. Either you'll drown or not."

Shortly after they bob off, and I go ashore to finish reading my book. Before I open it, I look up to see them bobbing across the horizon. They are indistinguishable, one from the other. One is wearing a white sun visor. But which one? I can't tell. I finish my book and gather up my things from the stony beach. I'm about to walk off and start packing my suitcase, when Thalia—mask atop his head and a snorkle in hand—stops me in my tracks with another of his jokes:

"An elderly man was enjoying dinner at a small taverna in the countryside with an elderly woman he'd just begun to date. He remembers the romantic taverna as the place he'd once brought young girls for seduction dinners long, long ago. When the moment would come, he remembers he'd take them behind this taverna, where he'd cozy up to the back fence, pull the girl close and begin to make love.

" 'How about taking a stroll outside into the back woods with me?' he invites his date.

" 'That sounds like a good idea,' she answers.

"There's a policeman sitting in the next booth listening to all this, and having a chuckle to himself because he knows that out back is where seductions take place.

" 'I've got to see these two old-timers trying to have sex,' he thinks, and follows them outside as they walk haltingly along, leaning on each other for support, aided by walking sticks.

"Finally they get to the back of the taverna that's full of flowers and trees and make their way to the fence. The old man presses the woman against the fence, puts his arms around her and kisses her deeply. Then he drops his trousers, lifts her skirt and pulls down her panties. Suddenly they erupt into the must furious sex that the watching policeman has ever seen. They are bucking and jumping like eighteen-year-olds. This goes on for about forty minutes! Finally, they both collapse against each other panting. The policeman is utterly amazed.

"It takes them about half an hour to recover. Finally the old couple puts their clothes back on. The policeman thinks that what he's seen was truly amazing; they were going like a speeding train. When the old woman goes off to find the ladies' room to tidy up, he decides to ask the old man what his secret is.

" 'That was something else!' he states, and asks, 'Did you know that's where all lovers go to make love?'

" 'Yes,' he answers, 'but I haven't been back here since I was a young man.'

"The policeman gushes, 'I'm amazed. You must have been having sex for about forty minutes. Tell me please, was there some sort of secret you learned all those years ago?'

"The old man replies, 'Fifty years ago that wasn't an electric fence.' "

I tell Thalia I'll see him in the spring and will be expecting a new quiver full of jokes.

"A little classier, please," I beg.

Then I climb the stone steps.

Determination

I go for a haircut to an apartment on the Upper East Side belonging to a hairdresser whom Barbara has touted. He does hair in a corner of his living room. Earlier in my life I would never have imagined in a million years that I'd one day color my hair, but I do. The hairdresser is sixtyish, cute, short, muscular and originally from Cuba. While he does my roots he tells me that he's just begun a new love affair.

"Do you care to talk about it?" I query, feeling like Kinsey.

I explain why I'm interested. So, while slathering a mixture of peroxide and dye onto my head, he obliges.

"Before it started, I was between boyfriends. I was lonely. I gained twenty-four pounds, drank a Grey Goose martini alone in front of the TV night after night. Well, more than one martini. All I could think about was that the clock was ticking away what was left of my sex appeal."

An acidic, cobalt-blue glob drips down my temple, which he wipes off with a cloth.

"In a state of self-pity—apropos of your interest—I'd compose personal ads to place in *Gay City* that said things like: *MINT CONDITION MALE, 1958, high mileage, some hair, some new parts including knee. Isn't in running condition, but walks with a snap in his heels.*"

He has me laughing.

"Or—*WINNING SMILE: Active older gent with original teeth seeking a dedicated flosser to share rare steaks, corn on the cob.*"

"Very funny."

"Mind you I never actually placed them in the newspaper. I sometimes imagined games for us older folk, like, musical recliners, sag, you're it, spin the bottle of Mylanta, kick the bucket. Want some coffee or tea?"

"Coffee. You're cruel."

He's finished applying the glop, and I must wait for the color to set. He turns an egg timer to thirty-five. I'm enjoying him and follow him to his minibar on which there's a coffeemaker. I notice a lacquered plaque propped against the liquor cabinet.

> One must console oneself with the thought that time is a sieve through which most of these important things run into the ocean of oblivion and what remains after this selection is often still trite and bad.
>
> —*Albert Einstein*

Seeing my interest, he picks it up and wipes it with the cloth he's still got in his hand.

"I've had this for years. Sometimes, needing solace, in that awful hiatus after another of my inevitable breakups twice a year, after the first martini, I'll look at it. Very quickly I feel justified in shaking up another martini and do. Get that look of sympathy off your face, you don't know me yet, my determination to find another lover wasn't dimmed. I turned over every rock, then hooked this sexy older guy."

The coffee's brewed and he pours me a mug.

"You're a funny guy."

"What I lack in looks, I make up for in wit."

I settle down again in the hairdressing chair with my coffee to wait and he sits on a piano stool.

"Not bad."

"I want to keep up with youthful trends, but don't you think we should avoid unbuttoned disco shirts and heart monitors, pierced tongues and dentures, nose rings and bifocals, bikinis if we have liver spots?"

He sees another drip on my forehead and wipes it off though I'm shaking my head and he wipes my eye instead.

NEVER TOO LATE

Newlyweds Robert Koch, 100, and Lena Kleine, 77, are all smiles after their wedding ceremony yesterday at a church in Grassau, Bavaria. The couple, who met at an age home several months ago, waited until yesterday so they could get married on Koch's 100th birthday. ASSOCIATED PRESS WIREPHOTO

"*Basta!* Oh, well. They say that life begins at fifty . . . or is it sixty? Maybe it's eighty? Ninety? One hundred?"

"So, in your opinion, was F. Scott Fitgerald wrong when he said that there are no second acts in American lives?"

"And how," he replies.

Three weeks later, when I come by for a touch-up, he tells me his new affair is kaput and that, apropos of our discussion on second acts in American lives, he's changed his mind. He has decided that Fitzgerald was right.

"And," he adds, handing me the plastic smock, "I've come to agree with Truman Capote who, if I remember rightly, said something like, 'Life is a moderately good play with a badly written third act.'"

He mixes the chemicals.

"Now here's one for you. Wilt Chamberlain, the basketball player, said that's it's harder to make love to one woman a thousand times than a thousand women one time. What do you think?"

"I think a thousand is a lot."

"Me too. I'm a love-hungry, tenacious kind of guy, but a thousand seems . . . well . . . how about five hundred?"

"To me it was a relationship of convenience"

The first thing Lillian Kohn tells me is, "I'm a man junkie."

Lillian is an outspoken woman, an electrical engineer who has lived on the Lower East Side of Manhattan for forty years. She was born in 1928 in Vienna, Austria. She admits that she isn't completely comfortable being taped.

"But I'll forget about it," she predicts, and it proves true.

Lillian and I have three breakfasts together at clone coffee shops called Moonstruck—one in the East Village, the other in Chelsea; all during a period of serial snowstorms that cripple the city. The city is digging itself out of the first one when I take the

subway to our initial meeting in the East Village. I'd called to suggest canceling, but Lillian—whom I haven't yet met—isn't
daunted by the weather.

"Don't feel obliged. We can reschedule."

Shamed, I of course tell her, "No, I'll be there."

The snow is deep. I have not seen a snowstorm like this since I
was in high school. I'm loving it. I tramp through calf-deep snow-
banks to the subway and get out at Second Avenue, then walk over
to First Avenue and up to Fifth Street. The snow has blown into
high drifts along an as-yet-untrammeled First Avenue. The city is
silent; a dream. Snow is stacked up on rooftops and fire escapes, giving the scene a Stieglitz-like black-and-white photographic quality.
When I open the door to Moonstruck, a blast of hot air envelops
me. The place is overheated. I notice a lively, ruddy-cheeked
woman of about seventy, with a cup of coffee in front of her, waving
me over to a large booth.

In 1990, Lee, Lillian's husband of thirty years, was diagnosed
with a heart problem.

"He never bothered to tell me. I thought it was asthma. He was
an avid tennis player. It happened in August. The heat was unbearable. He said he didn't feel well. The next morning I had a
race, a four-miler. You see I run marathons. I said to him, 'Should I
go? Are you feeling all right?' He didn't object, so I went to the race
like an idiot. When I came home, he'd gotten worse. He said, 'I
think maybe we should go to the hospital.' I asked, 'Should we get
an ambulance?' He said, 'Let's take a taxi.' We left the apartment.
At the elevator he admitted, 'I think I'm having a heart attack. My
arms hurt.' Then he confessed, 'I've been diagnosed with a heart
condition.'"

Her lips tighten.

"I got him to New York Hospital fast. He walked in and never came out. I called a friend, called my kids. It all happened in three or four hours. I used to think if you got to the hospital in time, then you'd stay alive."

Tears fall at this point. I turn off the tape recorder and give her time. The place is filling up. Everyone who enters stamps snow off their shoes and the area around the entrance is soaking with gray slush. Finally, Lillian wipes her tears away with a paper napkin. We eat hearty breakfasts and speak of other things. When the plates are pushed back and fresh coffee is poured, she says, "Let's go on."

Her eyes are sad and red-rimmed, but her voice is strong.

"I was really in bad shape after he died. I went to an all-women's bereavement group, which was helpful because women who had lost their husbands in unusual circumstances were in it. One committed suicide, another was gunned down in the subway. A couple of husbands died of cancer. All of these husbands died unexpectedly. It's a pretty awful ordeal to go through. It was a miserable time, but the group helped. They were women who I probably never would have met otherwise."

She chokes up again. I suggest, "Why don't we move along, talk about where you are now . . . the affair you're having."

"No. It kind of evolves better if I do it chronologically. By the time my husband died, I'd run about three marathons. I was running a lot, running well. I ran the NYC Marathon shortly after he died, in October 1990. I remember that part of the way through it I missed him terribly because my family had certain places where they'd meet me. My husband always stood and waved at me after I came off the Fifty-ninth Street Bridge, at Sixtieth Street. Then he and the kids would go to the park and be there when I came in."

She blows her nose, clears her throat.

"I kept thinking, He left me. He left us. He could have done something. He chose not to do anything . . . except die. He should have thought of his family, of how much we needed him. I was very angry with him even though I missed him. It was an ambiguous kind of thing. I remember coming in toward the finish line, through Central Park, thinking, Okay, he chose to die. I'm choosing life. It sort of carried me over the finish line."

When her husband had been dead awhile, she joined another bereavement group.

"This one had men in it. In it was a widower named Ernie. I thought it would be nice to have somebody to go out with. He had come to the United States about the time I came from Vienna. We eventually became a couple. It lasted for six years. To me it was a relationship of convenience. It enabled me to live the life I'd lived before . . . on the surface anyway. I could use my theater tickets. I could continue to get theater subscriptions, take trips. We used to go to art museums together. He'd been a stranger to art and he became something of an art expert while we were together. We went to Amsterdam, to the Van Gogh Museum. When we came out he told me, 'This is one of the greatest experiences of my life.' I'd opened up a whole new world for him."

She narrows her eyes.

"I don't know if this would qualify as love in the second act?"

I reassure her by saying, "It was an amorous relationship, wasn't it? It needn't compare to your marriage. It's not competing. Was it something comforting, something interesting, something that helped you get through the time . . . something companionable, sexual?"

Lillian nods.

"Ernie's wife had died of ovarian cancer. She went down pretty fast. He'd had a heart attack, then bypass surgery. He seemed strong. We traveled to Europe together. I took pictures. He looked great. But he started to have trouble with his heart. He went to the hospital in '98 but they let him go home. He died in his house. Nobody was there. His son tried to call him, didn't get an answer, broke into the house, found him sitting there dead. It was a shock but it wasn't as hard as when my husband died."

"I'm sorry."

"It left a void in my life. As I said, I'm a man junkie. I was determined to have a man in my life. So I started corresponding with men by computer. The thing that really drove me crazy was that I still had theater tickets, symphony tickets. When Ernie died, I renewed them. Why should I give up the theater?"

Before I met Lillian, Internet dating to me was reminiscent of the following story: In Madhya Pradesh State, India, two parties are on their way to be married. They arrive at Palon village. The brides' long veils are in place so the ceremony begins. First one bride circles the fire with her groom several times to seal the marriage. Then the second bride does the same circle seven times, sealing her marriage. Finally all brides and grooms have circled the fire. The veils are lifted. The brides discover that each has been married to the wrong bridegroom. The village elders confer while the brides and grooms wait. The elders tell the assembled: "In true Hindu tradition, once the seven perambulations around the sacred fire are complete, the vows are final." "But . . . but . . . but . . ." the bewildered individuals protest. "There can be no exchanges of spouses," the elder informs the new brides and grooms. "Go. Obey the law."

. . .

Our second and third meetings are at the Moonstruck on Ninth Avenue two blizzards later. The roofs I can see from my window are snow-covered. Downstairs I follow the trail made by various feet along the no-longer-pristine snow on Twenty-third Street. Plows have pushed the snow from the street into high mounds at the curb. Several cars are totally covered. I have to climb up hard-packed drifts and jump to cross the street.

I take an out-of-the-way booth and order coffee. Almost immediately Lillian joins me, pulling off layers of winter clothes as she sits down. We order breakfast. She begins where she'd left off, with the death of Ernie.

"Afterward I had some blind dates. I answered personal columns. The thing that would get me was that people would seem so interested. They'd speak with me on the phone. When they met me, they lost interest. I thought, Oh, well. I guess I'm too old. It's bad for your self-confidence. Some men in my age group were having an absolute ball with women much younger. Some women my age were having a ball with older men, or occasionally, younger men. In my quest for a theater companion I called a friend of a friend. This guy's wife had died in 1996. I told him my sad story. I didn't tell him that I'd called five other people, that everybody was busy and had turned me down. It was a Friday night. He said, 'I'll go look at my calendar,' which I thought was a bad sign, but he came back, told me, 'No no, I'm free on that night. I'll go with you.' I was overjoyed."

I call tell this meant a lot to her.

"We went to see the play. We sat upstairs. I don't remember the play but neither of us liked it. It was a flop. It seemed to me that we hit it off but I began to doubt my reaction because he didn't take me home, I took the subway by myself. But, when I got home, I got a phone call from him and he asked, 'What're you doing Saturday night?' So that sounded promising."

I ask what he looked like.

"He was short, had bad eyes and wore glasses. His name was Pete. We had similar political backgrounds. We also had a strong physical attraction . . . which hadn't happened in a long time. I wanted to do all kinds of things but he would limit me to once a week."

Our breakfast is served and I turn off the tape recorder. We jokingly trade lines from would-be Jewish personals that have been making the rounds on the Internet:

"Couch potato latke, in search of the right applesauce."

"Divorcé studying kabbalah, Zohar, exorcism of dybbuks, seeks mensch. No weirdos, please."

"Torah scholar, long beard, payos. Seeks same in woman."

"Divorced man seeks partner to attend shul with, light shabbos candles, celebrate holidays, build sukkah together, attend brisses, bar mitzvahs. Religion not important."

Lillian asks the waiter for more butter for her toast, finishes her cheese omelet and drinks a small glass of orange juice. We order another round of coffee and I turn the tape recorder back on.

"At the end of 2002, I wrote to someone on Match.com. He sounded pretty good. I went with this guy for almost a year. But in this case, I limited it. Truthfully, I was seeing this guy when I was going out with the guy who limited me. I once saw a movie where Billy Crystal was a basketball coach. He traveled, and his wife drove around with this dummy in the car next to her, so that she wouldn't feel lonely. Well, that's how I felt about a couple of these men I dated. I just had them around like a dummy. But I had a companion and that's what I wanted."

Lillian digresses. She takes me back to her childhood in Vienna.

"We were Jewish, but lived in a non-Jewish neighborhood before 1934. I didn't like being an only child, thinking of myself as an important person. My parents were overprotective. Once my mother brought a coat to school because it snowed, and it was very embarrassing. I was somewhat overweight. Fat childhood. Fat teenage years. Fat college years."

I ask, "Fat or plump?"

"Just plump. Being four feet ten inches, when I hit one hundred twenty-five pounds, I was chunky. Being Jewish, we had doom hanging over us. In 1938 Hitler marched into Vienna, he marched right under my house. It was a triumphant march, people lining the streets, people welcoming him. It was a formative time for me. My sensible father marched off to the American consul and began the long process of getting visas to America.

She sighs.

"He got tickets on a German ship. For some reason Jews could be passengers on a German ship at that time. It was called the *Hansa* and sank in World War Two."

She sighs again, then cheers up.

"I loved the ship. We went through a terrible storm. I remember going down the stairway, the ship rolling. There were only two other people in the whole dining room. Everyone else was sick. I was thirteen when we arrived in the United States. I was already interested in boys. Over-interested! I knew a little English, not

much. We lived in Washington Heights. Right away I did very well
in math. In America, the approach to boys was so different than in
Europe. My way of getting to boys in Europe was to get interested
in what they were interested in. I learned soccer and football, I
read boys' stories. I could talk to boys. Boys were not so chivalrous
as in Europe."

Lillian went to Julia Richmond High School, which was all girls.
She decided she didn't want to go to Hunter College, a girl's college.

"Somebody said, 'I'm going to City College and study engineering.' I was good at math. That's how I decided. Julia Richmond had
no boys; City College had no, or hardly any, girls. I went to City in
1943. My first year in City College I did spectacularly. It gave me
confidence. What do you do to become popular with boys? You
help them with math and physics. That's how I met my husband.
He was an accountant. We got married after World War Two and
lived in East Harlem. We were politically active. I started working
in the construction industry."

"A woman must have been a rarity in construction?"

"Yeah. I did electrical engineering. We had our son. Then our
daughter. He was crazy about the kids. It was a very good marriage."
She laughs, "The only thing I did to annoy him was to give birth
during tax season. Both my kids were born in March."

Her mood sinks again.

"We were married thirty years when he died of that heart attack. Anyway, we'll get back to Match.com when next we meet."

On meeting three, she begins where she left off.
"In 2003, after the last disaster, I went back to Match.com.
I answered an ad for a man who was a mathematics major. He men-

tioned that he had cultural interests. The only problem was that he was into sailing and wrote that he'd give preference to somebody who knew something about sailing. I knew I didn't qualify there. His politics . . . he said he was liberal. He lived in a town I'd never heard of on Long Island. He wanted to meet someone within sixty miles. It turned out he lived in Suffolk County, he'd put in sixty miles so he could include New York. He'd started out with twenty-five, but it turned out to be no good. After twenty-five he put in the whole country and met someone from California and realized that wasn't going to work either, so he made it sixty miles. New York is full of women."

They had a two-week-long e-mail correspondence. It started at Christmas. They didn't meet until January 4.

"We both wanted to see the Matisse-Picasso show. He wanted, of all things, to hear the Vienna Philharmonic. It was really a very nice program. They were doing Beethoven. So he came into New York, bought the tickets. The only thing that was wrong with him was that he couldn't walk more than a block without being exhausted."

"What was the matter with him?"

"He had angina. He was also one of these people who didn't go to doctors. He kept saying, 'I've got to do something about this.' But he never did. To make a long story short, he had a defective heart valve, had the operation. I was worried sick. I remembered my husband Lee—he was only sixty-seven. I remembered Ernie—he was seventy. Bill was seventy-eight. That's his name, Bill. He was no youngster. But he came through and recovered. The thing he said to me in the hospital was, 'I did it for you.' I thought, Well you don't really do it for somebody else . . . but I was touched. Even my husband wouldn't do it for me."

He recovered.

"He's fine. He can walk. He can walk a few miles. Unfortunately he still refuses to watch his diet . . . is still kind of cavalier about his health. He's the post-husband boyfriend that's worked out the best, which doesn't mean it's always smooth sailing either."

"Do you see him a lot?"

"I see him every weekend."

"You spend the weekends together?"

"Yeah."

"His place? Your place?"

"Mine. He's a pack rat; his is impossible . . . but sometimes his place. He's on the shore. He's got the boat."

"You enjoy his company?"

We get up to leave, begin our layering with sweaters, coats, scarves and hats. She continues speaking as she wraps a short knitted navy blue scarf around her neck.

"Yes. I go to the theater with him. His politics are okay."

The change comes and we walk out onto snow-covered Twenty-third Street. A few hesitating flurries are floating in the air, people are scurrying, trying to reach their destinations before the next blizzard begins. It reminds her of Vienna, it reminds me of childhood. In parting I ask, "What does Bill look like?"

"Age appropriate. I don't really like tall men. He's like five seven, gray hair, a beard. I have a lot of trouble getting him to wear decent clothes. He's very much into plaid shirts and jeans . . . but . . . if he needs a sports shirt for the theater, he'll say . . ." Lillian laughs, " 'What're you trying to do, make a clotheshorse out of me?' "

*"He's five years younger, which, at our
stage in life, I consider my age"*

I thought we'd meet face-to-face, but as it turns out, Flora Parker
is too busy to meet me. Instead she speaks to me from Fort Lauderdale by telephone. The tone of her voice is authoritative, no-
nonsense. It should be, she is a former family trial lawyer who is
now a judge. Though the Wilt Chamberlain quotation comes into
my mind, I'm slightly intimidated by Flora and decide against using
it to kick off our talk.

"Tell me what happened," I ask simply.

"Sure. In a nutshell, I engaged in Internet dating."

"Tell me more," I say.

"Sure. I was divorced about ten years ago. During the period of
being divorced, I had a series of semi-inappropriate relationships
where I dated much younger Latin men. I had a fabulous time. I
knew that this wasn't the sort of thing that would see me into my
old age."

"If you don't mind me asking, how old were you when you got
divorced?"

"I'll tell you anything. I was forty-five. I'd been married fourteen
years to a drop-dead gorgeous man who just wasn't a whole lot of
fun. It seemed like he wasn't going to provide me with the emotional availability that I wanted in a partner. It was hard to live
through life's pressures with someone who had a sort of depressed
spirit. When I was finally ready to search for a real-life partner person, it was with a different eye than I had ever had as a young person. After having had a man that every woman wants, you get to

realize that a pretty face alone doesn't do the trick. I thought, I'll approach this from an entirely different angle. Instead of looking for another pretty face, I'll try to find someone who seems to fit my requirements that are now different because I'm older and wiser."

I take my shoes off and listen.

"I started searching. First, anybody and everybody set me up. I told everybody that I was on the prowl. I went to a million jazz cocktail hours and other singles' events. I did churches. I did hotels with jazz clubs for singles. I did singles gatherings for those with advanced degrees. Uh-oh . . . roomfuls of all kinds of engineers with pocket protectors. I went out on five or six dates with each of maybe ten different guys I met through various Internet dating things. All of them were perfectly acceptable human beings. A couple misled me about their age or how much hair they had, but surprisingly, they were well educated, nice men. I didn't hit it off with any of them."

She speaks with logic and a calm tone.

"I'd curtailed my drinking twenty-three years ago and thought, Well, it would be nice to share that, so I got on a subsection of the Matchmaker website which is for sober singles. I wanted someone in a specific age range, someone who was self-supporting in a specific income range; I wanted a spiritual person rather than someone interested in devout religious activity or any particular order. I wanted someone who is African American like I am. There were a lot of things I could eliminate. I punched in all my search criteria."

Flora explains how the computer came up with maybe fifty men. Twenty or thirty were locals, two lived in the Midwest, and finally there was Chilton, the man she's with now, who was in San Diego.

"Chilton's profile ended with the line: *Looking for a girl who is near to my home. Not interested in long-distance.* I wrote anyway. The first line of my e-mail to Chilton said—*Not too close to home*—then I introduced myself. I proceeded to date some of the guys who were local, one of whom had a yacht in Palm Beach harbor. While I was busy dating, Chilton responded—*Well you couldn't be much further away unless you're standing on the water at the beach in Bermuda*—but we started to write each other e-mails, getting to know each other. We got to know each other very thoroughly by e-mail and we started to look forward to each other's e-mails. I kind of think of it like war brides or something like that. Then we started talking on the phone."

"How long did that take?"

"A couple of months. Neither of us took it very seriously but it started to get more intimate and more compatible. For instance we were both into spirituality. I've got boy children; he's got girl children. We were both parents and kind of understood. We seemed to be very, very similar. I hadn't ever really found a man who was similar in a comfortable fashion. He doesn't like sports. He cooks. There was a lot about him that was real user-friendly. We discovered a lot of the compatibility in the letters and then when we started talking we couldn't get off the phone—eight o'clock West Coast, eleven or midnight, East Coast. We'd still be at it. We'd speak for hours."

I put my feet up and stretch out.

"I was about to go to Thailand on vacation with one of my sons. We were talking on the phone and Chilton said, 'Well, I guess there's not much of a chance you'll be stopping on the West Coast?' I thought, What the hell, I've got airline miles, so I said, 'What if I break up the trip to Thailand and come for the weekend? I'll take Friday off, use my airline miles. We'll get it out of the way; we'll see each other, see if there's any chemistry?' He said, 'Fine.'"

I hear the click of another call on my call-waiting, but ignore it and continue listening.

"When I got off the plane, I had no idea who this person was. He didn't look familiar even though I felt like his spirit was familiar. He's a graphic artist. He had taken the Starbucks symbol and reproduced it into a sign like a limo driver. It said Flora alongside the Starbucks logo. He was standing at the end of the arrivals room. He laughed, said, 'All the other blind dates I've had I've met at Starbucks. But none came for the weekend.'"

I laugh too.

"He put me up in a lovely B&B in Encinitas where he lived. By the end of the weekend, he'd become physically familiar to me and it seemed like it was just meant to be. After my holiday, I flew home and we carried on a long distance relationship for a year. I went back there for Thanksgiving, for Christmas, for spring break. He came to Florida for two weeks. I took him on the grand tour from Miami to St. Petersburg, to my house and to my boat. Long story short, we fell in love. He sold everything he owned, home, car . . ."

"Teenage daughter?"

"Well . . ."

"I'm joking."

"Seriously, one of his girls decided to go back and live with her mother and he moved lock, stock and barrel to my place in Fort Lauderdale. As of this April, his daughter has come to live with us and do high school. We're officially engaged. And me having experience in the divorce business, I'd like to be engaged forever."

"Sounds fine."

"I recommend it to everyone. I found it such a sensible way to find a person. I read something that said women put more effort into finding the right pair of shoes to match a certain outfit than they do in finding a mate. I realized with me that that had been true. I'd never really gone interviewing for the position, if you will. It's really worked out great because we're compatible. He's a good communicator. We communicate with each other well. We have lots of things we like to share. We have a great time when we're together. He's affectionate and open. My boys like him. I love his girls. They're really open, sweet, lovely girls."

"Is he similar to you in background?"

"No. Not really. He was raised in Bend, Oregon. He's good to his mother. He comes from an intact family. He's family oriented. I'm from Atlanta but I was raised in Europe. I come from a flashy family. My father's a famous black chemist. He comes from laboring stock, a much quieter background."

"Is he your age?"

"He's five years younger which, at this stage in life, I consider to be my age."

"You've said a lot. Quite a promo for spending time, giving as much thought to looking for a mate as one does with one's shoes."

"I wouldn't have ever thought about the Internet if the girls in church weren't doing it. I first heard about Internet dating when it first dawned. I went to this rock 'n' roll Religious Science Church at the time. All the women were busy searching on the Internet."

"Matchmaker.com?"

"Uh-huh."

"Did you try others?"

"Uh-huh. I think I stuck with that one only because you can overload yourself. I just tried everything."

"About how long did this process take?"

"About two years. You know I'm a judge?"

"I do."

"When you say that in a bar to a single guy, it's not a turn-on. It's kind of like, 'Oh, shit!' So I think I'm a little harder to match up. I think a lot of high-end professional women are as well. Chilton's a self-employed graphic designer with a steady business. He designs textbooks, so the beauty of it is he can do his business wherever he wants."

"How long has it been?"

"We're finishing our second year. In August it will be two years."

"I like your story. Yours is an intelligent, lucid story . . . not about someone who was dropped on your doorstep gift wrapped. You used your brain, approached it logically. You set out to find what you wanted and did."

"Yes. We did. Chilt and I love to go walking along the beach at night. Afterwards we like to go for coffee and dessert to the Breakers Hotel where all the actors and actresses, old money, glamorous people from the past used to play . . . a romantic setting to say the least."

"I never thought of giving up"

The weather goes from bad to worse. My friend Barbara insists that I meet another of her friends, a man named Leonid Roth, and organizes a dinner party to coincide with his visit to New York. Leonid is a sixty-seven-year-old professor who specializes in Shakespeare and literature and lives in the Rocky Mountains. He's lived in the same eight-room house, built in 1914, for thirty-four years.

This house is surrounded by woods, a river and a snowcapped mountain. He has taught at the same college for forty-two years. Ten years ago he was diagnosed with, and operated on, for prostate cancer. He agrees to an interview and I go to his hotel the day after the dinner party.

"It was a great shock. I was devastated. 'Sickness' is a hard word for me to use. I was quickly convinced by my doctors that it was caught early and wasn't life-threatening. It was the sexual aspect of the surgery that was worrisome. They told me before the surgery that it would be a few months before I knew the sexual impact it would have. I felt like Job."

Born in Elizabeth, New Jersey, an only child, he had a happy childhood until he was eighteen and his father suddenly died.

"It was hugely traumatic for me and my mother."

Leonid went to Amherst and then to Yale graduate school in English literature. At Amherst a woman from Mount Holyoke named Susan saw him acting in a play based on the Nausicaa episode of the *Odyssey*. Leonid was Odysseus. He was virtually naked in the scene when Odysseus gets washed up on the beach. They met in a class at Yale several years later, dated and married. When Leonid was offered a professorship at a good western college, they went west together. The marriage lasted five years. He has never again married.

"The marriage wasn't deeply passionate. I got seriously involved with a student of mine. This was 1966, 1967. Sex, drugs and rock 'n' roll. I wasn't much past being a student myself at the time. In those days you could do those things with impunity. There was no such thing as sexual harassment. My college was quite liberal about such matters. My wife was somewhat placid; I'm passionate and energetic. Lucy, the student, and I had a tumultuous relationship that broke up the marriage. My wife later became gay. My relationship with Lucy lasted around four years."

For the next twenty-five years, Leonid had a series of relationships, none of which lasted more than four years. They were with artists, theater people, musicians, writers and other students. Leonid is very much a mature man with the body of a fit and healthy adult and a strong life-light. His brown eyes are luminous; they brighten occasionally while we speak. He is a very attractive man. I can see why women would respond to him. Leonid needs no prodding. He speaks in complete sentences. Quickly I realize that he won't have to be probed or questioned, so I lean back, sip my coffee, and—like a lecture presented by a confident lecturer—his story unreels:

"My pattern was to be monogamous . . . serially monogamous. Usually the women brokeup with me. My pattern would be deep regret after the breakup but lack of commitment and uncertainty during. I was in therapy a lot. Most of these women didn't live with me. I wasn't a commit-a-phobe; when women wanted more from me it wasn't marriage, it was some clarification that our relationships were going to go on. There were Diana, Fatima, Beebee and Mary Ellen. I was able to do lots of traveling during those years through my job. I taught in Egypt, had Fulbright lectureships in Hong Kong and Japan for a year each, and taught in Paris for long intervals on two occasions. All my breakups were deeply distracting. One was horrific. It happened in my middle fifties, well into the second part of my life."

He breaks stride and comments on how breakups in one's fifties sow the same havoc as breakups in seventh grade do.

"One of the two women I'd lived with was an academic— Marilyn. She had a two-year-old daughter. It was the first time I was around a young child. I was thrilled. I loved being with the child. I used to think, Most people have their children when they're young, I didn't. Now I'm going to have my child, in late middle age. I turned one room of my house into a charming playroom, another into her bedroom. I felt terrific about this."

"And?"

"Then my eighty-two-year-old mother got sick. For seven weeks she was in intensive care, and then she died. My mother's death coincided with the flourishing of this relationship. I remember an episode that happened soon after my mother died. I was on the floor with Marilyn; the child, Alice, came over and joined us. Then the dog Pepper came over and wanted to be included. We all rolled around in a ball and I was flooded with tears."

Leonid's eyes water as he remembers this incident.

"It comes back powerfully. It was my family, the kind of loving inclusion I wanted. I taught Alice to cook, I took her to plays and films, read her stories at night, talked to her. One day Marilyn met a man, a carpenter, somewhat younger than she. Within three days she decided that he was what she wanted for life and, when I was in Hong Kong, she broke up with me with a phone call which was to be about the arrangements for her and her daughter, age six at this point, to join me in Hong Kong."

He blows his nose.

"By phone! I was devastated. I'd never been in such a depression. I was totally paralyzed. I thought her treatment was horrific, ugly. The curtain had come down. It was so dramatic and psychologically violent. I realized quite soon that the loss of Alice, not Marilyn, was the great tragedy. Marilyn's the only ex-girlfriend I can't bear. Within five weeks of my return home I was diagnosed with prostate cancer. I hadn't had a single symptom. I'd gone for an ordinary physical exam, my PSA was elevated and I had an ultrasound followed by a biopsy. I'm glad to tell you that, for ten years now, I've been cancer-free. But, it's had sexual consequences."

At this point, Leonid goes off on a long detour about the modern drama course he teaches every year. I listen, finding it interesting, but realize that I've got an appointment in a few hours.

"Let's go back to your cancer. Did you have a sense that your romantic life was over?"

"I did."

"Were you with a woman at the time?"

"I'd just had the parting from Marilyn. But soon afterward a woman named Ellen came back into my life, an old girlfriend. She saw me through the worst stuff, including my birthday and Marilyn's wedding day. I didn't know for a few months about my sexual functioning, but soon it became clear to me that my erectile response was completely different from what it had been. I was convinced that it was going to be very, very difficult to be with a woman and there's nothing I wanted more. I was in therapy. The therapist talked in very sensible ways about other ways of being sexual. It certainly didn't entice me. It was so delicate; I'd have to find the right person who would accept me as 'damaged goods.' The first person I was attracted to . . ."

I interrupt him: "You're saying that physical attraction remained the same for you?"

"Oh, yes. There was no loss of libido. Orgasm is still fine. It didn't affect orgasm, it affects ejaculation, it affects erection. A year after the surgery I met a woman whom I found sexy and who also found me sexy. I remember telling her, 'I need to sit down and talk to you.' She thought I was going to say I was involved with another woman. When I told her about the sexual issue—it was before anything sexual had entered the relationship, it was a discussion to prepare her—she seemed very taken aback by it. She said she just couldn't be involved under the circumstances."

"Were you discouraged?"

"I was and I wasn't. I was very taken with this woman and she with me. I thought, Oh, my God. She seemed very, very right for me. We had common interests, we laughed at the same things, she's from the East Coast. A million things seemed right. She was decent about it. She wasn't cruel but it was very clear that this was not something she could handle."

He collects his thoughts.

"There are a whole series of ways to deal with the sexual problems—injections, vacuum pumps. Viagra hadn't come out yet. It was a year away. Nothing was working for me. I tried various things. Viagra, when it came out, didn't work either . . . it doesn't work for everybody. My feeling was that it was going to be difficult, no matter what."

"You never thought about giving up?"

"No, I never thought of giving up. It wasn't so much about sexuality per se, it was about wanting to be with somebody; to have a woman in my life to travel with, to talk to. I have a big, beautiful house, an old house. I know what it's like to live alone. I can do it well. I have lots of friends. I have almost no family. I've always wanted to be with a woman to share laughter, share insights and great talk. I love being in a room with a woman simply reading, and I love doing things together. I like an intimate, close relationship."

He continued to date. He'd meet an attractive woman, maybe a potential partner, and then he would have to sit down and say, "I've got to tell you something."

"On a couple of occasions, it was okay, but it normally didn't work out. I was never sure whether it was the sex issue or something else. Some women were very sweet, they'd say, 'It's not that.' But I was not convinced it wasn't. Then I met Clemmy. It's been my first relationship in my post-cancer time where the sexual relation has worked. We hit it off very quickly. On the third date it was the same conversation. Clemmy said, as others had said, 'We'll just have to see.' She didn't seem scared. She was loving and . . . there for me . . . from the start. I'd made dinner for her. We were in the kitchen. We embraced. She asked me to hug her. She gave a huge sigh and said, 'I feel as if I'm home.' And that was so huge to me. Metaphysically. Physically. It seemed like a very large gift."

His brown eyes meet mine.

"I've lived in the same house for thirty-four years. I've had the same job for forty-two. Perhaps the undecidedness of my private life has made it imperative to have stability and security in my job and home. Clemmy and I started seeing each other seriously. She's terrific. Oh, that's right, you met her at dinner last night. Sexually it's been very good, a kind of revival. With all the complications and diminishments physiologically, she's been very accepting and she thinks I'm highly sensual. We spent a month in Umbria. A month in Venice. Just returned from six months in Paris just now."

"You've been together a lot."

"Yes and it's been interesting. We had a huge apartment in the eleventh district. Lots of light. Paris is a wonderful place to live. I'm very happy when I'm there, though it's hard to work in Paris. Too seductive, too many distractions. Perhaps when I retire, I'll live six months in Paris and six months in the mountains. If Clemmy and I are still together"—he laughs—"in two years it'll be four years! You know me and four years!"

Time Is on Your Side

The wind is howling and raging outside, snow blows willy-nilly, spinning and whirling. I can see nothing from my window, it's a kind of whiteout. Several fire trucks race down the avenue, their gross sirens always unsettling. These heart-stopping dissonances that augur danger and emergency are the downside of being back in New York. Of being anywhere at all. The upside has been the long, bracing winter, the elation I feel every morning when I go downstairs and buy a container of coffee ("Light, no sugar!") from the vendor at my corner, Mohammed, who was born in Alexandria, Egypt. What seemed like a still-standing, cold heart early on in my return to New York, no longer does. Something inescapable, uneffaceable, has been weathered.

Between dozing and eating chocolates, I read a biography of Georgia O'Keeffe. It couldn't be cozier. At times like, storms and all, this I feel as if I've got the best life in the world. As I read, I'm struck by how O'Keeffe was a woman for whom age did not dictate her actions, who seemed to fall in love as deeply at ninety as she did at thirty. Alongside the reputation for overt sexuality in her work (her large-scale flower paintings evoke genitals of both sexes), she's known for an austere (some might say "severe") lifestyle: The tight knot at the nape of her neck remained unchanged throughout her life; she slept in a single, rather narrow, bed; ate her spare dinner at five-thirty in the afternoon and woke in time to see the dawn. ("You mustn't miss the dawn, it will never be just like this again," she said often.)

Georgia and Juan

Her relationship with the young man Juan Hamilton suggests that even at the approach of senectitude, the pleasures that she experienced remained keen. O'Keeffe's husband, Alfred Stieglitz, was born in 1864. Juan Hamilton was born in 1946, the year Stieglitz died. Both Stieglitz and Hamilton were dark, sensual men of talent with full mustaches. She was twenty-seven years younger than Stieglitz and fifty-nine years older than Hamilton. When she met Hamilton at the age of eighty-six and they began to live together, Stieglitz had been dead for twenty-seven years. Quickly her liaison with Juan became a source of concern to her heirs; he was accused of being a gigolo, an opportunist who was coercing an old woman for his self-ish gain.

O'Keeffe's plan to live to be one hundred years old fell short by two years. Until she died in 1986, in her ninety-eighth year, the bond between O'Keeffe and Hamilton held. Her capacity to sus-tain and maintain a deep attachment with another seems to have lasted to the end of her life. Near the end, when she recognized al-most no one, she still knew Juan and, according to witnesses, thought every man was Juan. When she called out, it was Juan whose name was uttered. Though only Juan and Georgia knew the truth of their liaison, Juan gave Georgia the best years of his youth, and Georgia gave Juan . . . well . . . everything. As per her wish, her cremated remains were scattered by Juan's hand onto the dry desert where, as Georgia had often said, "the sun burns through your bones." Her ashes joined with the desert sands to be blown by winds into drifts of mauve, blood-red, lemon-yellow layers that re-sembled the shapes in Juan's sculpture and the lines and colors in her painting. She'd had enough time for it all and more.

It's gotten dark. The storm's petered out. The new sliver of moon hangs alongside the golden crown at the top of the fifty-story Metropolitan Life building, about a mile distant from my window. The crown looks like a jewel floating in the sky. Below it, the clock's face is lit up in ivory splendor, projecting a translucent, floating sphere that renders the hands of the clock invisible from where I stand.

"We started to hold hands like so many
do when they meet, especially not knowing
what's going to happen. Seniors are always
such an unpredictable group"

My mother had been urging me, "Why don't you talk to my cousin Ruth?" My Aunt Roberta also urged, "You should speak with Cousin Ruth, ask her to tell you about Joe." So, in the middle of another day of lousy weather, I telephone my mother's first cousin—Ruth Metviner—who lives in East Lansing, Michigan. My mother had mentioned that when Ruth had first met Joe there had been a religious issue; they couldn't marry in the Church, they couldn't marry in a synagogue.

"Ruth?"

"Yes."

"Hello. It's Alison."

"We're just about to eat. No, no it's okay . . . that can wait. Here's Joe."

"Hello."

"Hello, Joe. I'm Alison."

"Well, Alison Wonderland."

"Right."

"That's what I keep telling Ruth."

"So your lunch is on hold while you talk?"

"Oh, sure."

"Mind if I tape you?"

"Oh, sure."

"Do you feel like telling me how you two met and what happened?"

"We have a 'Thirty-niner' group on the West Side of Lansing in the Waverly District, they call it. It's for the elderly, naturally, and I attended after Betty died in 1986, in June. Of course Ruth's hubby, Bernie—I mean, Ben—died the same year, 1986 . . . in April. After four years we . . ." (I can't make out his words) "Merged."

"Oh!"

"In 1990, they arranged a picnic and party for the seniors. I was sitting with a group of men, playing pinochle. One of the men said, 'There's a young lady looking at you.' I had a good hand at pinochle, which I wanted to play, so I said to Bernie, I mean Glen, 'Why don't you go and introduce yourself to her?' So naturally I had to turn around and look. I saw Ruth. She was smiling. The orchestra was playing. She was dancing with a guy named Bill who was married, so after about ten minutes, I walked over and asked her to dance. Bill didn't want to leave her until he finished the dance with her. And we've been together ever since."

"Wow."

"That's how it hits you . . ."

"Do you remember what the music was?"

"No, I don't, but it was a fox trot. Ruth and I just hit it right off. We started to hold hands like so many do when they meet, especially not knowing what's going to happen. Seniors are always such an unpredictable group. When you start to think how our good Lord has the common sense to combine the talents of two people . . . and so we did."

"That's fantastic. How long have you been together?"

"Well it was in 1990 we met, in May. Ruth did volunteer work for the seniors downtown. Right after Ruth and I joined hands I talked to a young priest about us."

Ruth and Joe

"And?"

"The priest said, 'Oh, we've got thousands of couples like you. You can iron out your difficulties and just stay the way you are.' Meaning, Don't worry about marriage, so that's what happened to us."

"May I ask how old you are, Joe?"

"Ninety-seven years old. It's incredible."

When he says ninety-seven with such verve in his voice, the image he conjures is of an ancient yew tree that has grown vertically in its youth and horizontally in midlife, and, even though its outward appearance has become twisted when it's old, the tree is nonetheless still producing new, living roots that feed on the soil, pushing down and down.

"It's wonderful that you found each other. It certainly is. What are you about to have for lunch?"

"We searched all over the place for early corn. We got stuck with field corn. It looked good. I should know better but I didn't. We have cold cuts, herring and borscht. It's so welcome for me because the Jewish community in Chicago always had such fabulous food."

"Is that your hometown, Chicago?"

"Yeah. Chicago is where I was raised. I'm a country boy who migrated to the big city. Ruth wants to say something."

He calls her. She gets on the phone.

"I want to tell you what he looks like. He's very handsome. He's six three . . . tall as Philip. You know Philip, my son? He's Polish-German. Beautiful. He really is. I kept looking at him. There were four men there and I picked him out. I said, 'This one's for me. Joe Boyer.' And I got him!"

"You were right."

"Yes, I was right. He's gray now. He was blond, blue-eyed; really handsome. . . . I just wanted to give you an idea. And, he's a nice guy."

"Do you live in an apartment?"

"No, no, no. This was Joe's house before . . . we live in a house. We have a little house and a front yard, a backyard. The kids of Philip and Wendy gave us a beautiful glider which Joe calls a swinging bench. And, we have a very good, a very happy life. Very quiet. We don't do too much."

"You do everything for yourselves?"

"Yes, we do. Joe has a large family. I have Philip, Wendy and the children. I'm ninety, Alison. Ninety!"

"The trophy wife."

We both laugh.

"My birthday's on December 7th . . . like your father. You may find someone more interesting than us."

"I doubt it. I better let you have lunch."

She calls out, "Joe, say good-bye."

Again there's a moment of silence while the phone is passed back to Joe, who says, "Good-bye, Alison Wonderland."

"Happiness sneaks in through a door you didn't know you left open"

The owner of the Arbor suggested that I speak with her sister, so—before too many months have passed—I'm sitting on the back deck of the Mansfield-Greenwald family home, in a small town just outside of New York City on an unseasonally mild day at winter's end. After only fifteen minutes with this family, I think of a Milton Berle line (purported to have been said to him by John Barrymore) that happiness always sneaks in through a door you didn't know you left open. Below me, preparations to plant the garden have begun. Several trees have been delivered and sit beside the house, their roots wrapped in burlap. Boxes of geraniums are waiting to be planted. There's a sprawling lawn and a driveway on which are two exquisite, life-affirming little girls riding tricycles. One girl is about four and the other about seven. A small creek and stand of tall hickory trees mark the boundary of the property newly owned by this family of four, or five, if the male parakeet named Mary is included. When they'd all gathered at the front door to greet/peruse me a short while ago, Mary had flown straight out from his cage. He cut through the air like a buzz saw, barely missed my hair, then circled back directly into his cage.

Speaking first with David Mansfield about his marriage to Maggie Greenwald, he tells me, "Marriage seemed to be the natural next step. It seemed to be a way of having a celebration of something that had happened naturally. I think we both had feelings that we'd met our soul mate."

They are in their late forties and met when he interviewed for and got the job of composing music for a feature film she'd written and would soon to direct.

"I'd had a long career at that point in writing music for films when I went to meet the director. I don't recall preparing for the meeting . . . it was just another job. The subject matter of the film and style was similar to work I'd done before. I was a natural fit."

Their relationship started as a creative collaboration, but began to change when they were working intensely during the last stage of the film (in postproduction) and the hours started getting longer.

"Were you creatively compatible?"

"Yeah. Very. Things started to shift one night when we went out to grab a bite together after finishing work. As I recall, it was a slow turning. I realized that we had a lot in common personally, and I thought that was a good thing. The romance built up to a tipping point. We both realized we were having feelings that went very fast; we had a real love affair. It went on for a year and a half, could have been two years, before getting married."

Until the age of forty, David told me, "I gave the impression of still being a child. I had always looked young, had been precocious in my work."

In past years he'd had long hair and looked like a rock 'n' roll musician. At fifteen he was a performing musician, by seventeen he was recording for a major record label; by twenty-one he'd toured the Western world, had already gotten a lot of attention for his creative talents. (David had been a member of Bob Dylan's "Rolling Thunder Review" and had composed music for *Heaven's Gate*, *Songcatcher*, *The Apostle* and *Divine Secrets of the Ya-Ya Sisterhood* among many others.) It wasn't until gray began to appear at his temples (yes, that's really where his began) in his mid-forties that he stopped wearing his hair long; "I didn't want to look like an aging hippie."

At a young age, David married, fathered a daughter he adored. He shifted from performing music to writing in order to curtail traveling to be with his daughter.

"Were you a natural father? Or did you find it a role you had to work at?"

"In hindsight, I was very natural about it. I loved it. I was a very involved parent."

My attention is drawn to a deer standing below us in the garden munching the geraniums. I point it out to David.

"They're frequent in that yard this time of year. They're fawns . . . spotted fawns. They're all over eating everybody's gardens. They're not very popular with the flower lovers."

Shortly, Maggie takes David's seat so he can light the barbecue. She sips green tea.

"What's he cooking?" I ask.

"Lamb, I think."

As David begins to load briquettes into the barbecue, the children abandon their tricycles, join him on the lawn. Quickly, lighting the barbecue becomes a family event.

"I've observed your family and it seems to me you're very happy. Would you agree?"

"It's nice to hear this. We are very happy. My husband and I became parents at an older age and have an intense appreciation. We love every minute of it. We do have a really great time together."

"Why don't you tell me a little about where you are right now."

"I live in a beautiful small town not far from New York City. I have a husband and two sensational children. I'm a filmmaker with a moderately successful career."

Maggie's being modest. She's an accomplished writer-director of several award-winning films that include *Ballad of Little Jo* and *Songcatcher.*

"Tell me a little about your history, who you were emotionally and in matters of love. Who you were in act one of your life?"

"I was a driven artist, totally committed and dedicated to my work creatively and professionally. I had lots of friends but had lived a very constricted life with regard to relationships. I avoided—was afraid of—any kind of long involvement, fearing it would interfere with my work. I didn't travel either. I was afraid to take time off. I was very unhappy because nothing creatively—professionally—was ever good enough."

"Vices?"

"My main vice was that I was a heavy smoker from age thirteen through thirty-one. Two and a half packs of cigarettes a day. One of the things that was the beginning of a huge change in my life was when I quit smoking. Part of why I quit was because I had the feeling it was interfering with living my life, not just my health but also my emotional thing. I was living under a cloud of smoke. About fifty cigarettes a day. Lighting up every fifteen minutes. I'd been living in Los Angeles but had moved back to New York. I was so unhappy, I don't think I had a real vision of my future."

David has finished lighting the barbecue and disappears into the house. So do the children.

"Did you find getting older easy or difficult?"

"I paid much too much attention to it, found getting older difficult. I'm the youngest in a family of four children. I went from always feeling that I was too young to feeling that I was too old."

"What about children? Did you want them?"

"When I was a kid, I loved children and wanted lots of them. By the time I'd become an adult, I'd become very cynical about relationships, about marriage. I was very certain I'd never marry, certainly never thought I'd be in a long-term relationship. I figured that some day I'd have a child and I'd raise it alone or with the help of a nanny."

I thought of these recently clipped lines written by Sylvia Brownrigg:

For those of us who've never known the state [of being married] it sails past us like a cruise ship, lamps all on and parties raging. We wave from our smug or perhaps lonely shores, waiting till the sea-scattered brightness has withdrawn its silvery music and we're left alone in the dark, on dry land, to carry on with our unfettered midnight explorations.

Maggie continues: "My deep emotional unhappiness . . . I was very depressed, filled with despair most of the time. I had an instinct that without more life experience, my work wouldn't grow and change, wouldn't have maturity, grow deeper. I had the feeling I'd make the same film over and over."

"Did your creative vision start to broaden as you hoped?"

"Yes, it did. My work was initially very dark . . . bleak. As I opened up emotionally I moved away from being focused on darkness to being interested in deep feeling and character. I became more positive. In an effort to change myself and change my life, I became involved in very, very intensive psychotherapy of different types to help me become capable of really becoming involved with someone else. As a young woman I had a very, very negative attitude . . . anger . . . at men, which thwarted my involvement."

Lulu, the younger of the girls, appears at the doorway.

"Hi, Lulu!"

"Hi, Mama. A big bug came in my room . . . a big hole in . . . uh . . ."

"The screen. Did Daddy get it?"

"Dad-da!"

She climbs onto Maggie's lap.

"It was moving on my window. It went onto my book. Daddy wiped it off and threw it in the garbage. Me and my Dada didn't want anyone to get stinged . . ." She slithers down from her mother's lap, explains, "I go for a bike ride."

She dashes down the steps, across the lawn, past David who has returned to the barbecue holding a platter of meat and mushrooms and fresh vegetables. He lines up various foods on the grill with long tongs. Lulu runs to her tricycle, gets on and pedals up the driveway.

"Tell me about your first meeting with David."

"I loved his work. I had no particular impression of him when I met him."

There is a pause as we both turn to watch Lulu. She lopes like a sumo wrestler, the sight of her is comedic, making us both laugh out loud.

"He was slight, he was dressed quite conservatively. He was quiet. He seemed a little distracted. He wasn't in the same rhythm as everybody else. We were all having a lot of fun. He kept to himself. It wasn't until five months later that I became attracted to him. He wasn't around the shoot but was when we began to screen cuts of the film. One day David got off the elevator and walked toward us and I went, 'Oh, my God!' I was suddenly really attracted to him. I felt like I was seeing him for the first time. It wasn't too long afterward that . . ."

"Cupid struck?"

"That's one way of putting it. Within a short time I realized that I wanted to be with him for a long time, and fortunately so did he. I think falling in love really informed the piece of work we were making together."

The older child, Maisie, walks regally toward us, holding a hairbrush.

"I have a knot."

I ask, "You like when your mommy brushes your hair?"

She nods.

Maggie takes hold of the hairbrush. "You have a few little tangles. There you go. I'll come up later and wash your hair."

Our eyes follow her. She is tall, slim and steps lightly; her shoulder-length hair was tied up with bright elastics when I arrived. Now it falls freely.

"We kept our affair a secret for a short time. But we couldn't stay away from each other."

"How was the film received?"

"It was a critical success and a box-office disaster. It was in festivals and theaters all over the United States and in Europe. By the time it opened, we'd decided to live together. We were together every night anyway. We got married the following summer. The idea of children came up early on. I panicked because the film hadn't done well commercially. I just panicked and thought, Gee, maybe I should just wait until I make one more film? I didn't understand that I could do both at the same time."

"Your biological clock?"

"We started trying when I was forty. Within a year I had not conceived. We went to a fertility specialist . . . but let me backtrack. Before I made the film, I felt that I wanted a child. That time was growing short. I'd met someone who'd had involvement with adoption in Cambodia. I decided that when I finished my film, I'd adopt a child on my own. Then I met David and thought we should have a child . . . and, if I wanted more, I could adopt. While researching adoption I became aware of the plight of all the abandoned girls in China. I'd always been attracted to Chinese culture. I thought it was extraordinary. There was something about all those little girls that moved me beyond anything. So while we began the fertility process, we also began investigating adoption. I had always, from the time I was a little girl, wanted to adopt. From fourth grade, I felt that that's how I'd build a family."

Maisie stands near the barbecue and watches.

"I knew that even if I conceived, I'd proceed with the adoption. Then it became obvious that I couldn't conceive, so I went full tilt with the adoption process. There was certainly some grief about not being able to have a child, but it was not significant. By this time, I wanted a child more than anything. It was all I could think about through the year it took for our names to come up. When we were called, we didn't get a picture, we got a name and a place and a birth date. We were expecting to get a baby that was over a year old so I had gone and taken a course in Chinese so I could speak with my new daughter. When we finally got the call, we were told she was only five months old. Her birthday was in December. Her orphanage name was Xiao Biao, which means Small Strength."

The emotion is infectious.

"I would have to say that the two most amazing experiences of my life have been the two trips to China to be united with my daughters. If I were younger and richer, I'd do it regularly. There's a feeling for me and for anyone who adopts . . . a feeling of fate."

"Of going to meet your fate?

"Hmmm . . . going to meet my fate and somehow or other a higher power—the universe—is connected. Something greater than me was connecting me to a child I'm meant to be with. I don't think I know one person who's adopted who doesn't have the feeling that they ended up with the baby they were meant to be with."

"Amazing."

"We packed a huge bag full of diapers, three kinds of baby formula and toys and clothes. We had shots even though they weren't required. We went with twenty-four other families to Guangzhou, China, and then we split up because some were going to different areas to get children. We went with eight other families way into the south to a small city called Maoming, which is about three hundred miles from the Vietnamese border, near the South China Sea."

Lulu dashes down the steps and joins David and Maisie at the barbecue.

"We were taken to the town notary's office. The notary in each town is the legal person who officiates at the adoption. Each parent or couple—there were numerous single parents—was asked to come up and then the baby was brought."

Her eyes are brimming with tears; she chokes up. "I can barely talk about it without crying. . . ."

She smiles and cries at the same time.

"Others were in front of us. I was sobbing. Some people received babies. It wasn't private, it was a shared experience. I cried for ten days. I was overwhelmed by how amazing this was and what these children had been through. Here were all of these parents who were as desperate for a baby as these babies were for a parent."

David walks over, carrying a platter of barbecued meat and

vegetables. The children have gone off somewhere. He adds to the description:

"It was an amazing moment. Here's the person, she's laid in Maggie's arms, and she's just looking at us, amazing, beautiful, big, wide, dark eyes that said, 'Who are you?'"

"Was she swaddled?"

Maggie replies, "She wasn't swaddled. The place in China where Maisie's from is very hot. It was summer, really hot. She had on a diaper and little pajamas. They had bought new clothes for the presentation. I've saved those for her."

David and Maggie exchange long looks.

Maggie continues, "I was sobbing, and the three of us were just looking at each other. We had to move off to the side because it was the next family's turn. I always felt bad for the last family. No one to take pictures for them."

David adds, "And then we went to the notary's office and filled out the papers."

Maggie continues, "We were invited to visit the orphanage where she'd lived. I thought that it was really, really important for me to photograph everything for her; that this would be the only record she'd have of where she spent the first five months of her life. David held her and through endless tears I photographed everything. Everyone was very, very sweet, the women who'd taken care of her. They had put litchis on the table. Very moving. Out front, I'd never seen so much laundry in my life, drying on racks . . . probably a million diapers."

David adds, "It was very intimate, very emotional, a dreamy experience. These families were mostly close to our age, some a little older, some single. The thing that was so striking about it was that here were these people who'd spent a lot of time thinking about adopting. This made it different than being around a younger new parent. There was an intense fulfillment happening that was quite amazing. A lot of the people there . . . dreams were being fulfilled. It wasn't just young people having babies."

He beams as he continues.

"Our baby was very serene . . . looking at us . . . had a very connected gaze. We were struck by how beautiful she was. For those first few days, we spent a lot of time just looking at her. We were amazed by her. She was very easy. A lot of the children have minor medical problems—rashes, parasites, upper respiratory infections, lice or eczema. Even the best orphanages are poor. Ours had almost no problems, just some eczema. She was perfect. All we had to do was feed her, change her and enjoy her."

"How long was the flight back to New York?"

"It's a grueling trip. Twenty hours—I can't remember now—to Los Angeles, then on to New York. But it was actually quite easy. We splurged. I made up a little crib on a big business-class seat with pillows. She just snuggled down and slept the majority of the flight."

Maggie continues, "We went back three years later as a family. Brought Maisie. This time it was winter."

"Was the second one as emotional?"

David replies, "Yeah. It was very emotional. It was the same. We had the briefest little glimpse into Lulu's life before we got there because the foster mother brought a couple of favorite foods—little mandarin oranges, clementines—some eggs, some formula which was very sugary, treats and little squares of angel food cake, like Mexican supermarket cake. I'd better bring the food into the house."

But before he goes, he explains: "Lulu had been cared for by a farm family in the city of Fuzhou. It was an elaborate presentation process. The foster mother and Lulu had been behind a screen. The foster mother handed the baby over to Maggie and helped comfort her, let her know that she was handing her over to someone trustworthy, that she wasn't being taken from her. Lulu cried. The foster mom said a couple of words to her in Chinese. Over the next few days she was sad and grieving but she wasn't hysterical or panicky. What the woman did in the ceremony helped our daughter."

He carries the tray up to the house.

Maggie explains, "This was a different part of China. She had these big round cheeks. Her orphanage name was Qina [pronounced *Chee-na*], which means Cute Girl. It was wintertime, in a cold part of China. She was swaddled in six layers of clothing. She had split pants on. I didn't realize how little she was when she was presented to us . . . she was eleven months."

"What did the foster mother say about Lulu?"

"That she loved to sit outside and watch the ducks. She loved ducks. Her first word in English was duck. She told us she loved clementines."

"How was Maisie?"

"I wasn't focused on her but she was fascinated by her new sister. She was right there. She was interested in Lulu's split pants . . . and that she could see her tooshie through the pants. I think so much of the transition into our family being so smooth is because of Maisie. Maisie embraced her completely, was very loving and wanted to hold her and helped me change diapers, gave her her first bottle. She was very, very excited, gave her her first nickname when she was noisy—Loudy—and because she has these round, apple cheeks—Dumpling. For those first months, Maisie called her Loudy Dumpling."

"What's your life like now?"

"I have a three-and-a-half-year-old, a six-and-a-half-year-old. After September 11th I thought living in New York City was too

Mansfield-Greenwald Family

difficult with two kids, and a year ago we found a wonderful little town that we fell in love with. It's very unique, diverse, progressive community and very beautiful. We moved here. I'm living a life I never would have imagined. Living in the suburbs with a husband and two children. My interests recently are children's clothes, swimming lessons and gardening."

She laughs.

"My work in these years has gone very, very well. A year after Maisie came home, I made another feature film which has been wonderfully received but television films give me a chance to work regularly, to work as a craftsman. I've worked on a huge variety of projects and I've earned a nice living for the first time in my life and stopped struggling."

"If the twenty-five-year-old you came over and sat down with you now, what would she say to her?"

"The twenty-five-year-old would need an ashtray. I don't know. She would probably envy and disdain who I am now. She would be completely shocked and amazed. I didn't think . . ."

She pauses, watches Lulu and Maisie running onto the lawn together, playing tag or some such.

I attempt to fill in her reply, "That there was a place for love in your life?"

Maggie smiles at me.

"Love is everything. Sorry to be corny."

"Of course."

"For me, family life means more to me than anything."

Lulu runs over. She's wearing a pink-and-blue dress and swirls around proudly. Then she pulls me by the hand. "Daddy says come inside."

We go through the kitchen and pantry to the dining room, where David is putting the last touches on a large salad. He uncorks a bottle of wine. Then we sit together at the large oak table and eat grilled lamb, grilled portobello mushrooms, grilled peppers and large scoops of delicious salad that includes lots of mushy avocado, slices of scallion and florets of broccoli mixed in a tasty dressing.

"Why is this dressing so delicious?"

"It's got the usual garlic, balsamic vinegar, olive oil but lots of soft, overripe avocado that's bordering on rotting . . . and the secret ingredient is a bit of honey."

We eat like hungry wolves. Being around the children is like inhaling whiffs of opium. The dessert has been assembled by Maisie, who has decided she'd like to be a chef. It's whipped cream cake— whipped cream, chocolate cookies—in alternating layers. She regally carries it to the table with a smile that could light up the darkest vault and, with Lulu's help, cuts elegant slices of cake. After dessert, the children go into the family room to watch a video of *Shrek*. Maggie goes back into the kitchen to prepare coffee and teas.

I ask David, "You're almost fifty years old. As one who felt so young for so long, how do you feel about starting to have some distance from a youth that seemed as if it would go on forever?"

"I feel so much better about this time of life. Things have changed in the last couple of generations. If people are in good health, one gets old much, much later than one did a couple of generations ago. And starting a family in one's middle and late forties—in my case it's really a second family—it's a perfectly wonderful time to do it. In fact, we've each accomplished enough in our careers over the years that we're living quite comfortably and our struggle is to maintain a nice lifestyle. It's no longer the struggle of just getting our basic needs met."

The girls return for second helpings of cake.

Maisie asks us adults, "Would you like more cake?"

We don't resist.

David continues, "The big thing is having the experience to be reflective, be very conscious of what we're going through, the things we're enjoying with our children, with each other, with the family. Even our lifestyle in our big hundred-year-old pseudo-country house."

Mary the parakeet shoots across the room, makes a sharp U-turn and flies back to his cage.

"The downside, like every age, has its challenges. This one is that you start realizing for the first time in a profound way that time isn't unlimited. You start to get much more realistic about goals and aspirations for a career to get a greater awareness of mortality. The depth of experience to enjoy this very intense phase of life which—having a new or young family—is unparalleled. Especially to be able to enjoy that in one's forties and fifties."

Maggie brings hot coffee and tea to the table; we sit together, satiated, pleasantly so.

ENCORE

Last night the sinking sun turned the glass windows in surrounding high-rises and offices to molten, fiery gold. I watched the windows blaze until the sun sank low enough for the fires to go out. When the last light of day remained, I was struck by a vague image of my face in the glass. Oh, no! I leaned in to get a closer look. In doing so, though the image was still vague, that feeling of being on a turbulent airplane nonetheless returned. Sure enough it wasn't me in the glass. But who else could it be? I looked more closely and, odd as it seemed, I was seeing the face of Helen Mirren. Sort of. Helen Mirren with a different nose, different hair and different eyes, but a face nonetheless that had something about it that's Helen Mirrenish. The feeling of disequilibrium passed. I could live with that face, I thought. Then I went to bed laughing at my own bad eyesight.

Today, in the little park below, buds are fat on the London plane trees, and the Bradford pear trees that line the street have exploded into white blossoms. Because it's breezy, the blossoms have blown helter-skelter. Like strewn confetti or rice after a wedding, the entire sidewalk and street is speckled white. I'm surprised when winter unexpectedly returns for an encore. Suddenly thick snowflakes fill the sky, blowing up rather than down, depositing a dusting of dazzling white on rooftops, on parked cars, on tree limbs, on the benches and on the grass in the park. The blossoms decorating the street get covered up, as do the minute shoots of crocus and daffodil that have just broken through the earth's surface in our little park. Although I have a few more interviews to do, my traveling symposium is complete. My literary leaning toward darkness and war has been diverted . . . for now.

A friend who's visiting from Los Angeles stops by for a drink. She hasn't expected snow and is wearing strappy sandals. She's enchanted by the white wonderland, so we stand in front of the window admiring the whirling flakes. I don't know if she realizes that she's looking at the place where the Twin Towers once stood.

"There's a building that looks like a sand castle," she points out.

I'd never seen the downtown skyline that way before but it's not a mirage; she's right. I fill our glasses. My friend has brought a sack of fat pink peaches, so I find a ceramic bowl and pile them in. She's just celebrated a "big" birthday—seventy. Sotto voce, she asks, as she twirls a downy peach, "Do I dare to eat a peach?"

She takes a bite and laughs. We carry our glasses out onto the enclosed terrace and sit down.

"I've heard all about your book," she tells me.

"Oh!"

"Apropos of sex among us over a certain age, I thought this information might be useful: A couple my age, seventy, go to a sex specialist's office. The doctor asks, 'What can I do for you?' The man says,

'Will you watch us have sexual intercourse?' The doctor looks puz-zled, but agrees. When the couple has finished, the doctor says, 'There's nothing wrong with the way you have intercourse,' and charges them $50. This happens several weeks in a row. The couple makes an appointment, has sex with no problems, pays the doctor, then leaves. Finally, the doctor asks, 'Just exactly what are you trying to find out?' The old man says, 'We're not trying to find out anything. She's married and we can't go to her house. I'm married and we can't go to my house. The Holiday Inn charges $90. The Hilton charges $140. We do it here for $50 and I get back $43 from Medicare."

"Very funny."

"Long live Medicare!" she adds, raising her glass.

For the remainder of the afternoon we drink coffee and catch up on births, deaths, divorces, marriages, illnesses and recoveries. Good news and bad. World news and gossip. Before she goes off to the ballet, she hands me a brown and black glass turtle the size of a golf ball.

"A terrapin," she tells me, but noticing my stupefaction adds, "A terrapin's a small turtle."

"Oh!"

"I'll show you what you do with it."

She rummages in my kitchen cabinet for a saucer, wets it with a few drops of water from the tap.

"You must put it in water. It must face north for good fortune and a new love."

She stands the turtle in the water, and places the saucer on a bookshelf.

"You're not against finding good fortune and new love? Or it finding you? Are you?"

I think of Andre, Odile, Lillian, of Terrence and Tom, Louis and Margarita, Beatrix and the others. And then Cicero's prophecy in *De Senectute* passes through my mind:

> I am wise in that I follow the good guide nature: it is not likely,
> when she has written the rest of the play well, that she should, like
> a lazy playwright, skimp on the last act.

My dear friend turns the retractable head of the terrapin to face north before I can say, "How could I be against all that?"

Photo Credits

All efforts have been made to secure permissions for all materials in this book.

1. Andre, photo by Tony Kahn, courtesy of Andre Gregory
2. Tom and Terrence, courtesy of McNally/Kirdahy
3. Ayrin, Michelangelo, Joyce and Dan, courtesy of Dan Fante
4. Sister Cheryl Donahue, courtesy of Cheryl Kane
5. Cheryl and Jim—Act II, courtesy of Cheryl Kane
6. McDonough-Trang Family, photo by Alison Leslie Gold
7. Jane Mayhall, photo by Peter Kayafas, permission Peter Kayafas
8. Tessa and David, courtesy of Chantal "Tessa" Dahl
9. Patricia Neal, courtesy of Patricia Neal
10. Mother and Father, permission Alison Leslie Gold
11. *She and She*, courtesy of Olga Kusaková
12. Maggie and Stathe, courtesy of Martin/Dekavallas
13. Wedding of Tony and Mary, courtesy of Gladstone/Church
14. Wedding of Marianne and Jan, courtesy of Marianne Christine Ihlen
15. Marianne at seventy, photo by Helge Eek, courtesy of Helge Eek
16. Wedding of Pandias and Lila, courtesy of Pandias and Lila Scaramangas
17. "Never Too Late," Associated Press, Wirephoto

18. Georgia and Juan, photo by Don Budnik
19. Ruth and Joe, courtesy of Ruth Metviner and Joe Boyer
20. Mansfield-Greenwald Family, courtesy of Mansfield-Greenwald Family
21. Alison Leslie Gold, author photo by Thor Gold, permission Thor Gold

Acknowledgments

My appreciation to the authors, translators and publishers who gave their kind permission to quote from their works:

Sylvia Brownrigg, *Pages For You,* Picador, Macmillan Pub. Ltd., London 2001.

Constantine Cavafy, "Candles," translated by Robert Liddell, from *Cavafy* by Robert Liddell, Simon & Schuster 1974.

Jane Juska, *A Round-Heeled Woman,* Villard Books/Random House, Inc., New York, 2002.

Milan Kundera, *Immortality,* translated by Peter Kussi, Faber & Faber, London, 1991. Used by permission of Vera Kundera.

Philip Larkin, "Faith Healing," from *Collected Poems of Philip Larkin,* copyright 1989, used by permission Farrar, Straus & Giroux, 1999.

Jane Mayhall, *Sleeping Late on Judgment Day,* copyright 2004, Alfred A. Knopf, permission of the author.

Plato, *The Symposium,* translated by Christopher Gill, Penguin Classics, London, 1999. Copyright © Christopher Gill, 1999.

"*Sam, You Made the Pants Too Long.*" Words by Fred Whitehouse and Milton Berle, adopted from "Lord You Made the Night Too Long" by Sam M. Lewis and Victor Young. Copyright © 1932, 1940 and 1966 Shapiro, Bernstein & Co., Inc., New York. Copyright renewed. International copyright secured. All rights reserved. Used by permission.

Sy Safransky, "Some Enchanted Evening," from *Four in the Morning*, The Sun Publishers, 1993.

Wallace Stevens, "Final Soliloquy of the Interior Paramour," from *The Collected Poems of Wallace Stevens*, copyright 1954 by Wallace Stevens, renewed 1982 by Holly Stevens. Used by permission of Alfred A. Knopf, a division of Random House, Inc.

Paul Theroux, *Dark Star Safari*. Copyright 2003. Used by permission of Houghton Mifflin Company.

Thanks to: Samuel Beckett, Milton Berle, Lois Smith Brady, Charlotte Chamberlain, Marcus Tullius Cicero, Wilt Chamberlain, Leonard Cohen, Albert Einstein, T. S. Eliot, Katherine Emmet and James Peterson, Rabbi Malka Drucker, Jeffrey Hogrefe, F. Scott Fitzgerald, Martha Horton, Giuseppe Tomasi di Lampedusa, Terrence McNally and Thomas Kirdahy, Sarah Mahoney, Gerry Margolis, Jane Mayhall, Helen Mirren, Eva S. Moskowitz, Elaine Schecter and David Herscher, David Steinberg, *The New York Times*, John Rice, George Seferis, William Shakespeare, Stevie Wonder, Dylan Thomas, Oscar Wilde, Robin Williams. All efforts have been made to secure permissions for all materials in this book

For special help: Maureen Connell, Danielle Durkin, Darin Elliot, Louise Fishman, Thor Gold, Dan Gunn, Kristina Kovacheva, Olga Kusáková, Barbara Lapcek, Kate Lardner, Marijane Meaker, Sharon Smith, Sheila Talcott, Mark Walter.

Solidarity with those who cared for, and contributed to, this book, especially my agent, Leslie Daniels; my editor, Sara Carder; and all who are trying to keep hope in our hearts as we walk on, walk on, through mutating storms.